"*Women Who Marry Houses* is a wonderful, highly percep- tive, and much needed book. It goes beyond its own study of agoraphobia to enlighten us about the female condition." —**Phyllis Chesler**

"*Women Who Marry Houses* is an important, deeply needed book which sheds light for the first time on why millions of women decline to leave their place: the home. Women who have ever felt unwelcome in the world—those barred from Little League as girls, subjected as youths to campus rules never applied to men, sexually harassed or underpaid on the job, fearful on the streets at certain times, denied admittance to clubs and golf courses, i.e., all women—must read this book."—**Gena Corea**

"Seidenberg and DeCrow have done a mind-boggling analy- sis. This book argues persuasively that agoraphobic women are protesting their female role, voting with their bodies. Ago- raphobia becomes the archetype of all the social, psychologi- cal, economic, political, as well as physical restrictions which make women fearful of the outside world."—**Jessie Bernard**

"It is ironic that women who once were not allowed into the *agora* are now labeled sick if they cannot go to the market. A strength of this book is its combination of feminist and legal thinking, and its trenchant criticism of the overuse of drug therapies in psychiatry."—**Pauline B. Bart**

"Once again we are presented with an important work that demystifies so-called 'feminine' behavior. By imaginatively focusing on the seemingly remote problem of agoraphobia, Seidenberg and DeCrow help us, with startling clarity, to un- derstand the devastating and damaging consequences of so- cially enforced sex roles. Eighty-eight percent of all agoropho- bics are women; the remedy lies neither in nature nor psychology. If women are to participate fully out of doors, in politics, economics, and art, they must exist in a world which truly accepts equality between the sexes. Seiden̶ Crow feel it is time for a chang̶ —**Florence Rush**

WOMEN WHO MARRY HOUSES

WOMEN WHO MARRY HOUSES

Panic and Protest in Agoraphobia

Robert Seidenberg
and Karen DeCrow

McGraw-Hill Book Company
New York • St. Louis • San Francisco
Toronto • Sydney • London • Mexico • Hamburg

Grateful acknowledgment is made to the following publishers for permission to quote from their works:

Harvard University Press: *The Poems of Emily Dickinson* ed. Thomas H. Johnson. Cambridge, Mass.: The Belknap Press of Harvard University Press, copyright 1951, © 1955, 1979 by the President and Fellows of Harvard College. Reprinted by permission of the publishers and the Trustees of Amherst College.

Houghton Mifflin Company: *The Life and Letters of Emily Dickinson* by Martha Dickinson Bianchi, copyright 1924 by Martha Dickinson Bianchi, copyright renewed 1952 by Alfred Leete Hampson. *All My Pretty Ones* by Anne Sexton, copyright © 1962 by Anne Sexton.

Random House: *The Glass Menagerie* by Tennessee Williams, copyright © 1945 by Tennessee Williams and Edwina D. Williams, renewed 1973 by Tennessee Williams.

1 2 3 4 5 6 7 8 9 F G R F G R 8 7 6 5 4 3

ISBN 0-07-016284-0 {H.C.}
0-07-016283-2 {PBK.}

LIBRARY OF CONGRESS CATALOGING IN PUBLICATION DATA

Seidenberg, Robert.
  Women who marry houses.
  Includes index.
  1. Agoraphobia. 2. Women—Mental health.
3. Sexism. I. DeCrow, Karen. II. Title.
RC535.S45 1983 616.85'225   82-14934
ISBN 0-07-016284-0 (hard)
ISBN 0-07-016283-2 (pbk.)

Book design by Janice Willcocks Stern

Some women marry houses.
It's another kind of skin.

ANNE SEXTON

We are both fortunate in being able to dedicate this book to our mothers, whose confinement made us, and ultimately this book, possible.

To Juliette Abt Lipschultz and Rose Carmen Seidenberg, with love.

CONTENTS

Acknowledgments

The authors are grateful to Susan M. Wood, law librarian of the New York State Supreme Court for the Fifth Judicial District, for her generous help in locating relevant cases.

Our warm thanks to the following people who supplied us with much useful material: Judith Brigham, Peg Cameron, JoAnne Fisher, Dr. Julian Franklin, Paula A. Franklin, Charles Gellert, Lois A. Kriesberg, Dr. Louis Kriesberg, Claudia Abt Lipschultz, Juliette Abt Lipschultz, Rowena Chaiton Malamud, and The Rev. Betty Bone Schiess.

Our thanks also to the typists of the manuscript: Tina Bielecki, Marion Cole, June Cull, and Margaret Soukup.

We are filled with admiration for our editor, Cynthia Merman. Not only did she understand what we were trying to say, she aided us in saying it more coherently and more cogently.

With gratitude to Dr. Evangelos Papathomopoulos of Athens who helped clarify the nature and functions of the *agora* of ancient Greece, and to Faith A. Seidenberg, a pioneer in the legal struggles to make restricted public places in contemporary America accessible to women.

Lastly, our devotion and our thanks to our agent, Elaine Markson, and her associates Geri Thoma and Sheryl Dare. Without their perseverence, constancy, and tenacity we would not have had the pleasure of having this work published.

Introduction: The Streets Still Belong to Men

Western society is a product of the Judeo-Christian tradition. From antiquity, the message of where every woman belongs is clear: "The man must master his wife, that she go not out into the market place, for every woman who goes out into the market place will eventually come to grief."*

Philo of Egypt (20 B.C.–50 A.D.) depicted the physical restriction of Jewish women: "Women are kept in seclusion, never even approaching the outer doors, and their maidens are confined to the inner chambers, who for modesty's sake avoided the sight of men, even of their closest relations."**

Married women were limited as much as possible to the household, and unmarried women limited even further: "The women are best suited to the indoor life which never strays from the house, within which the middle door is taken by the maidens as their boundary, and the outer door by those who have reached full womanhood.†

Women were not to show themselves off like vagrants in the streets before the eyes of other men, except when they had to go to the temple: even then they should take pains to go not

---

* Genesis, Rabbah 8, 12, in Leonard Swidler, *Women in Judaism: The Status of Women in Formative Judaism* (Metuchen, N. J.: Scarecrow Press, 1976), p. iii.

** Flaccus, 89, in ibid., p. 214.

† De Specialibus Legibus, III, 169, in ibid., p. 214.

when the market was full, but when most people had gone home.

The greatest measure of a man's virtue was his control over his wife, especially over her public activities. Rabbi Meir (ca. A.D. 150) said: "As men differ in their treatment of their food, so they differ in their treatment of their wives. Some men, if a fly falls into their cup, will put it aside and not drink it. This corresponds to the way of Papus b. Judah who used, when he went out, to lock his wife indoors. Another man, if a fly falls into his cup, will throw away the fly and then drink the cup. This corresponds to the way of most men who do not mind their wives talking with their brothers and relatives. Another man, again if a fly falls into his soup, will squash it and eat it. This corresponds to the way of a bad man who sees his wife go out with her hair unfastened. . . . Such a one it is a religious duty to divorce."*

In Palestine at the start of the Christian Era, unmarried women were kept indoors. Married women's public appearances were limited, and where they were allowed to venture out, their heads and faces had to be covered. There was a quasi-harem existence in Palestinian Judaism of the first century A.D. In Alexandrian Judaism, the harem conditions were even more stringent. When a Jewish woman went out in public, her head and whole face were covered, with only one eye free. To go out without a head covering was so shameful that it was grounds for divorce, and some rabbis even considered divorce mandatory.

Jewish women were not only severely restricted on the street, they were in general to be heard and spoken to as little as possible: "He that talks much with womankind brings evil upon himself and neglects the study of the law."** Rabbi Hisda (ca. A.D. 300) went further. A man should not converse with a woman on the street, not with his sister or even with his wife, because not everyone knows who are his female relatives.†

* bGit. 90a, in ibid., p. 214.
** Aboth, 1, 5, in ibid., p. 216.
† bBer. 43b, in ibid., p. 217.

Among the Slavonian Jews it is the custom to make circles on the walls of the bedroom with coal or saltpeter in order to protect a woman in childbed against wicked spirits. Pregnancy, of course, has been called "confinement" in many cultures; motherhood has constituted cultural confinement in practically every society. What of fatherhood?

Couvade is a primitive custom in which the father of a newborn child lies in bed for a certain period, eating only prescribed foods, abstaining from severe work (from the hunt, for example), while his wife, who has just given birth, carries on her usual occupation. Different origins are ascribed to this custom. A religious interpretation is that couvade is a remembrance of original sin, and the isolation and rules of abstinence are signs of deep repentance. A more materialistic explanation is that couvade is a symptom of the transition from maternal authority to paternity, and emphasizes the father's part in procreation as opposed to the "mother right" that originally existed. The father pretends to go through confinement in order to obtain the right over his child that earlier belonged only to the mother.*

One thing we know for sure about such confinement is that for the male it is temporary, lasting only hours or, at most, days, in contrast to the decades of encirclement experienced by even the most liberated mother.

Obviously, much progress has been made since the days of the ancient Hebrews. Laws and customs have changed dramatically. But it is still very much a part of the human record, there to be found within us. We need not invoke such concepts as "racial unconscious" or "phylogenetic recapitulations" to understand the power of history. In our enlightened, liberated times, most of Judaism still will not ordain women as rabbis. Questions about their purity remain.

For those who believe that these cruel imbalances, if relevant at all to the modern world, act only as distant Jungian memory traces, we draw attention to a group of more than a

---

* T. Reik, *Ritual Psychoanalytic Studies* (New York: Farrar, Straus and Giroux, 1946), p. 58.

hundred thousand women in New York City in 1982 who are victims of Orthodox Jewish marital practices and of course their own beliefs. These are women who obtained civil divorces but cannot be freed from their husbands because under Orthodox Judaism only the husband can grant the bill of divorce, or *get*. If he refuses, the woman cannot remarry or even date. She must remain in a state of imposed social estrangement pending his will or whim. Such a woman is known as an *agunah*, an "anchored-down" wife.*

Agora is the Greek word for marketplace, a considerable open space within the walls, the political, social, and commercial focus of the community where farmers brought their produce for retail sale, where business agents met their clients and associates, and where popular assemblies were convened.

Agoraphobia, as we use the word today, still deals with the marketplace. It is an incapacitating anxiety on traveling away from the presumed safety of the home. Between 5 million and 20 million people in the United States have agoraphobia. Eighty-eight percent of them are women; most of them are married women.**

In Greek times, "proper" women were excluded from the public domain; courtesans were the only females seen on the street. So we are faced with the paradox of woman, who was originally prohibited by law and custom from entering public areas of activity, and who is now diagnosed as *phobic* when she becomes anxious there.

Today a woman with a desire for a public life is burdened by many frustrations, social and psychological penalties, and gross inequalities of actual opportunity. Traditionally, hers has been the private sector; the *agora* was never a place where

---

* Georgia Dullea, "Orthodox Jewish Divorce: The Religious Dilemma," *The New York Times,* July 5, 1982.

** For further data, see L. E. Burns (U.K.) and C. L. Thorpe (U.S.), "National Survey of Agoraphobics," *Journal of International Medical Research,* supplements 1(132) and 5(1), (1977).

she was expected to be or where she expected to feel comfortable.

The limits placed on females in our culture are extensive. All women incorporate these limits in some form or other into their perception of themselves. Trauma and panic can arise from conditions less obviously threatening than a confrontation with lions, or tornadoes, or muggings in the street.

People can be afraid not of some specific or general event that may happen, but of the fact that in all probability *nothing* will happen. So it is with the agoraphobe.

We decided to write this book after an article appeared in *The New York Times Magazine* that missed the point of why people, especially women, and most particularly the women featured in the article, might be agoraphobic.* The subhead of the article, "To millions of Americans victimized by their own panic, self-help therapy and drugs offer new hope of cure," gave the impression that these intrusive modalities were legitimate "cures" for the "disease."

The article discussed the fear of "losing control," but did not explore those very few situations in our society where women actually *have* control. It described the panic of one woman: "When she gave birth to a son, she wanted to be in the psychiatric instead of the maternity ward." There was no understanding that a woman—educated, financially well off, good-looking—might have real fears about motherhood, about bringing forth a son who could do most things in the world denied her. There was simply a discussion of the drugs she was given and whether or not they "worked."

Finally, the patient submitted to the therapy of two experts, worked with a "helper" (a third-year doctoral student in psychology), and was "cured" in four months. Apparently finding the cause was irrelevant to the cure. Having ignored the cause, we learn that the cure consisted of various field trips with the helper—to amusement parks, tunnels, airports, places of special terror for her.

* Julie Baumgold, "Agoraphobia, Life Ruled by Panic," December 4, 1977.

We believe that in a culture that has consistently doled out punishment to women who travel away from home (from unequal pay in the workplace to blame for children who turn to drugs to actual physical assault on the streets), it is no surprise that certain women, sensing the existential irony of their situation, refuse to leave the home. We see agoraphobia as a paradigm for the historical intimidation and oppression of women. The self-hate, self-limitation, self-abnegation, and self-punishment of agoraphobia is a caricature of centuries of childhood instructions to women. One can no more "cure" the agoraphobe than one could "cure" the cartoonist Herblock.

We are critical of both behavior therapy and drugs as cures for agoraphobia. Only when society gives just value to the work women do at home, and makes it easier for them to leave the home to do fully accepted and compensated work, will women no longer need to be agoraphobic.

Few secular colleges today have curfews for women. But within recent memory such restrictions were part of campus life, while male students blithely came and went from their quarters at all hours. At first, women were excluded from higher education altogether. Then, finally admitted, they were treated like children, not only with curfews, but having to sign in and out of the dormitory. In many schools today men may live where they please but women must live on campus.

Restrictions imposed on one sex and not the other not only serve to induce and reinforce fears but also inform young women that their freedom on the outside is limited.

A dramatic clue to the understanding of agoraphobia is found in employment. The sex segregation of the job market, in addition to keeping women economically dependent on men, serves to deliver the more dangerous, subtle message: Women are really not fully welcome in the workplace. Although more than half the women in this country have jobs outside the home, the difficulty of getting into previously male-only jobs makes it clear that women who break the barrier are not wanted. Affirmative action programs, important as they are, are a Pyrrhic victory if the beneficiaries are there as a result of a federal shotgun at the head of the employer. The fact of the necessity for affirmative action is not lost to the sensibilities of women.

Agoraphobics may well be the most completely uncompromising feminists of our times. They will not be placated or bribed by small favors or grants of limited access. Sensing that they are not welcome in the outside world, they have come to terms with their own sense of pride by not setting foot on land that is deemed alien and hostile.

1

Marriage and the Agoraphobic

DECLARATION OF DEPENDENCE

A woman who was independent, self-sufficient, and capable married and suddenly experienced a drastic personality change. With no apparent reason the former blithe spirit developed "phobias and other signs of constriction of self."* She became helpless and underwent an almost complete change of life. She became fearful of traveling, frightened of being alone, and unable to make any decision or take any responsibility on her own. She clung to her husband for constant support. Dr. Alexandra Symonds, the psychoanalyst who treated this woman, noted her change from a strong person to the classically helpless female. At the same time many of the patient's previously held interests and talents were completely given up. She suffered a series of psychosomatic complaints that kept her internist and gynecologist busy. Depression became her steady companion.

Dr. Symonds believes that for such women, marriage is not the broadening and maturing experience that it is purported to be; it may in fact have the reverse effect of limiting and constraining. For these women, marriage has become a Declaration of Dependence. The first stage of this process occurs when a previously capable, often highly educated and perhaps professional woman marries and immediately gives up her work and settles for anonymity. She becomes "a paragon

---

* Alexandra Symoinds, "Phobias after Marriage, Women's Declaration of Dependence," *American Journal of Psychoanalysis* (1971). The term "Declaration of Dependence" is attributed to Dr. Carl A. Binger.

of Victorian femininity . . . helpless, housebound, and ineffectual."

Dr. Symonds postulated that after marriage the phobic woman described above became fearful of being *in* control, fearful of setting her own direction, moving on her own, exploring and discovering. This responsibility agoraphobes abrogate.

In the abandonment of control, Dr. Symonds finds a defect of personality stemming from childhood: "As girls they were capable and self-reliant but were not really whole." She detects an early lack of resiliency that takes its toll later in life, especially in marriage.

That people come to marriage with varying degrees of preparedness goes without saying. However, this given should not deter the examination of the marital state itself as possibly causative in the undoing of certain people.

Sociologist Jessie Bernard writes that marriage places a greater emotional strain on women, that "traditional marriage makes women sick—both physically and mentally." In every marriage relationship there are two marriages: the husband's marriage and the wife's marriage. The husband's marriage is generally a beneficial one; it enhances his mental health, happiness, career success, income, and life expectancy.* The wife's marriage, on the other hand, is a destructive one. Married women are more depressed, have more nervous breakdowns, have more feelings of inadequacy, and are generally less healthy, both mentally and physically, than single women. Dr. Bernard sums it up: "Women are driven mad, not by men but by the anachronistic way in which marriage is structured today—or rather, the life-style which accompanies marriage today and which demands that all wives be housewives."**

* For a discussion of these issues, see the papers from the National Congress for Men conference, Detroit, Michigan, August 1982.

** Jessie Bernard, *The Future of Marriage* (Cleveland: World Publishers, 1972), pp. 3, 72.

The silent inequities in marriage demand greater compromise and renunciation on the part of women than men. If a woman does not acknowledge these inequities, then she has no choice but to believe that any feelings of oppression she has are a figment of her neurotic and childlike imagination.

Dr. Symonds treated a thirty-eight-year-old woman. She had been referred by her internist who labeled her seriously depressed and physically run down. Married for eight years with two children, she felt she was a failure as a wife and a mother. She and her husband had sex rarely, perhaps once or twice a year, because he was impotent. She took the blame, which he heaped upon her, maintaining that she loved him. In Dr. Symonds's experience it is characteristic of these patients to accept uncritically the most outlandish attacks upon themselves. This is consistent with the patient's need to maintain the picture "of a weak, helpless woman being pushed around at home by an inconsiderate and aggressive husband."

At the same time the woman may also be well aware of her own culpability in allowing herself to succumb to the marital state in the first place: a state that would mentally humiliate and degrade her, as perhaps she had seen happen to her mother or sisters. This must, of course, be left unspoken since most women have been allowed no rhetoric in this area.

This woman's phobias developed gradually, she did not recall any abrupt or precipitating event. Yet she could no longer use an elevator, enter a subway, drive a car, or travel by plane without experiencing unbearable panic and anxiety, in contrast to her premarital days when she had owned her own car and enjoyed traveling to distant places on vacation. Now she was practically housebound. Her insistence that she loved her husband and had always wanted to be married and have a family was typical. Rarely and only exceptionally can a woman allow herself the luxury of any other belief.

Another patient of Dr. Symonds similarly came to her as a medical referral, having suffered from severe anxiety for three or four years with headaches, palpitations, sleeplessness, gastrointestinal distress, and feelings of impending doom. She had been married for ten years and now had a two-year-old child.

Unlike the previous patient, this woman recalled a sudden onset of her phobias: They first occurred eight years earlier when she and her husband were traveling, on a trip that the woman had insisted on taking against the wishes of her husband. She prevailed at the time, but the very next day she became terrified at the prospect of flying on a plane, making the remainder of the trip a horrible ordeal. She felt that her "aggression" had played a significant role in her subsequent illness.

Apparently taking control—even momentarily—was her undoing. Thereafter all travel became almost impossible. When she forced herself to travel she experienced nausea and vomiting. An educated, intelligent woman, she became angry at her apparent weaknesses, calling herself stupid. In addition to the severe restrictions on her mobility, she suffered distressing physical symptoms, as well as insomnia.

Prior to her marriage, she too had led a life of independence and autonomy, as much as the world allows women. She had been a nurse in charge of a ward in a large hospital and was easily able to handle her complex responsibilities. When she married, she was expected to, and did, renounce her profession. Now she was incapable of performing the simplest executive task. She did indeed look stupid. But did she perhaps secretly mean stupid for having renounced her profession, with its pride and opportunity for control and independence? In the metaphor of travel, did she stupidly relinquish the chance to find out how far she could go in her work and in the world?

Dr. Symonds notes that these women generally come from families where "self-reliance, independence and control of feelings are necessary, where there was little tolerance for childlike interests." As a result, these women had to grow up in a hurry. From early childhood they developed skills and qualities that gave "the illusion of strength." As teenagers and young women all of them acted cool, capable, and self-sufficient.

Dr. Symonds has made an enormous contribution in this area of emotional disability as it affects women. Dispensing with the deadendedness of conventional Freudian psychoanalytic theory, which says that marriage is woman's only valid success, she highlights the woman's dilemma of integrating shaky foundations of the past with an almost impossible present. Dr. Symonds was among the first to understand that women who declared their dependence, represented here by severe illness and disability, were making a social and political statement that awaited a feminist third ear to comprehend. And the marital state itself, heretofore considered almost sacrosanct as a developmental imperative, is shown to be as much in need of analytic scrutiny as its celebrants.

THE MARRIAGE IMPERATIVE

They found Debbie in a cemetery adjacent to the college campus. Just in time: She had been comatose for several hours, apparently the result of an overdose of tranquilizers and sleeping tablets. Brought to the emergency room of the infirmary, she was revived although already in shock and close to death. After several days in the intensive care unit, she was allowed to resume her normal activities with the stipulation that she seek psychiatric help.

Several weeks prior to the suicide attempt Debbie had visited the same infirmary complaining of acute episodes of palpitations as if her heart were bursting out of her chest. She had the subjective feelings of impending death. She was examined, reassured that her heart was in good condition, and given tranquilizers. She also received sleeping pills for her chronic insomnia. The attending physician spoke of "senioritis"—a supposedly common malady of students about to face the cold, cruel world outside. The medication "worked"; the palpitations diminished. But Debbie's troubles proved to be more complex than the obvious physical complaints.

Although Debbie resented the suggestion that she needed a psychiatrist, she dutifully made an appointment. After the preliminaries, she told the therapist that she was not crazy and if her symptoms were, as he believed, due to nerves, she couldn't identify anything that was troubling her.

When he asked if there had been any recent changes in her life other than impending graduation, she noted that she had just broken off with her steady boyfriend of two years. He no longer wanted to go steady with her and told her bluntly that he was disappointed that she was no longer the 100-pound sophomore he had taken up with. They had been sexually active together to her satisfaction but now, because of her weight gain, not to his. He would like to continue as friends but he could make no commitment for the future. She couldn't tolerate such an arrangement; when she decided to stop seeing him altogether, he put up no protest. She was bitter for a while but convinced herself that is was a good riddance—a girl has her pride!

But Debbie was sure that she had gotten over this disappointment and didn't see how it related to her present situation. She was most willing to be treated symptomatically for her physical disturbances. Perhaps the answer was a different drug for her self-diagnosed biochemical imbalance. Even before her initial visit to the infirmary, she had tried megavitamins as well as a full panoply of herbs and natural foods that allegedly restore the body to its normal state. And, after her boyfriend's complaints about her weight, she had gone on various diets, even to the extreme of induced vomiting after eating. These measures generally failed; they led to orgies of ice cream, potato chip, and Coke binges between meals. She remained obese—to herself; by conventional standards she was indeed quite attractive. However, after the breakup with her boyfriend, there was little time or opportunity for the flowering of a new serious relationship. She had occasional dates but most men on campus were already committed to others or were preoccupied with job interviews and plans for their careers.

She now seemed socially defeated, especially compared to the ebullience of her classmates who were getting married, engaged, or coupled. She tried to persuade herself that she was lucky to be looking forward to an immediate future without the impediment of an attachment to some selfish, ungrateful guy. She would then see herself as liberated from a male and a confining and debilitating fate. How close she had been to giving up her freedom!

Furthermore, there was her own career. She had majored in design and planned a career in the fashion industry. Now she could devote full time to her designs without being distracted by the needs and demands of a boyfriend or husband. Debbie wasn't especially interested or active in the feminist movement, but she was conversant with the issues of self-development for women as a primary concern, even ahead of getting a man.

Debbie had been brought up in a traditional household in a small town. Her father was a pharmacist, one of the few left who owned his drugstore. Her mother was a devoted housewife and mother whose main venture into the outer world was helping out occasionally in the store. The household also included her maternal grandmother, who helped with the chores and the raising of the children.

Debbie lived in the shadow of her sister, six years her senior. The latter did well in school and won a scholarship to college. She matriculated in the school of home economics, met a fellow right off, and was married during her sophomore year. She never graduated, but since her husband came from a wealthy family her parents considered her a success. She quickly had children.

The family had little expectation for achievement for either daughter. On visits home during vacations, Debbie was reassured that she was as attractive as her sister and would also find a man who would appreciate her. Debbie was not so sure now after her boyfriend's blunt and cruel rejection. According to her parents' values, she came home empty-handed after their investment in a college education.

Despite denying any despair over the rejection, Debbie found it increasingly difficult to leave her dormitory room. Although she was able to attend classes, she suffered severe palpitations and feelings of impending death in social situations, on her occasional dates and at parties.

She expected some degree of loneliness and exclusion, but it seemed incomprehensible to her that physical pain could be caused by personal unhappiness. Her family offered her support, reassuring her of their continued love and that she was in no way a disappointment to them. At the same time they suggested that it wouldn't hurt to lose a few pounds and offered to pay for a Weight Watchers program. This program, which included exercises in behavior modification, did not bring about either the promised weight loss or increased self-confidence.

Debbie blamed herself for neglecting her body and for lacking the social graces attractive to men. It was all her own personal failure. Hadn't her parents given her every opportunity, including an expensive college education? The contrast to her sister's seeming success only made matters worse. Yet, even though she acknowledged her unhappiness, Debbie could not see a relationship between it and her physical agony. Now almost any event outside of her room brought on the symptoms. Yet she continued to insist that it was her disordered body that caused her distress, not the reverse.

She was greatly relieved when her therapist told her that she had agoraphobia: "You see, I knew that there was something wrong *with me* and not a case of nerves." For her at that time, as for so many others in this predicament, having a disease is reassuring. It sounds like a medical problem, for which there may be a cure or remedial program at hand instead of a need to explore and face painful social and psychological realities. No wonder so many agoraphobics have been easy prey for quick-cure clinics and programs that promote this deception, encouraging patients to forget about their lives in order to overcome their agoraphobia.

As the rapport ripened in therapy, Debbie seemed to gain some hope and optimism about her plight. She began to see a relationship between her life and her symptoms—no small feat for agoraphobics, who generally deny connections.

Debbie was filled with guilt about having been a disappointment to her family; she added to her guilt with a suicide attempt. And she lamented that she couldn't even succeed at that! Her memory of her suicide attempt was clouded, but did reflect the irony that a person who for six months could barely leave her dormitory room because of fears of impending death should in fact seek death in the open spaces of a cemetery. She was beginning to reflect on the complexities and ambiguities of the human condition. This was something new for her. At college she fitted in fairly well, smoked occasionally with her boyfriend, and accompanied him to football and basketball games. She never gave much thought to feminist issues, didn't care one way or the other about the Equal Rights Amendment, abortion, or job discrimination. These had never been discussed at home and she hadn't attended meetings or rallies on campus where she might have learned about them.

Debbie had been intent on adjusting well at school and preparing for a traditional future. This in turn meant that she was entirely happy, or so it seemed, with the idea of a life of dependence—as her grandmother, mother, and older sister apparently were. These were her only female role models. She was beginning to see what a social calamity her boyfriend's behavior had wrought. She was perplexed and bewildered by this turn of events. What do you do after you have done all the right things?

Although she did succeed in masking it, underneath she was seething with rage at the injustice done to her. It was the emergence of these feelings that she feared in subsequent social situations, as well as the fear of more injury, that turned her into a recluse. As the therapy progressed she saw for the first time the inequities of social rules and mores that put women at a distinct disadvantage.

Her role seemed one of deference and submission, vulnerable to whims and fancies. She discovered that women weren't judged by inner beauty, loving kindness, or devotion, as her mother and grandmother had told her they were. It was a competitive market. People were bought and sold by the pound—the leaner the better; and a few pimples could mean more to the fate of a relationship than the most intense passion. This, Debbie perceived, was something women endure; men are largely exempt.

The outside world (of objects) did not treat Debbie kindly, and she came to view it as a hostile and inimical place. These insights came to her slowly and painfully. She was so accustomed to blaming herself for her deficiencies and failures, she had been so carefully indoctrinated in a woman's responsibilities by well-meaning relatives, that it was difficult for her to recognize how unfairly she had been treated and how this precarious mating position is the lot of most women.

The therapy lasted three years, during which time she made considerable progress in "reordering her priorities." Although she continued to hope that she would find a man who would appreciate her, she paid more attention to her talents and possibilities for a career—with no encouragement or support from her bewildered family. She found work in the clothing industry in a metropolitan area. She was still not completely comfortable in the outer world but enough so to continue her career.

Now at the age of twenty-six she is still unmarried. However, when last heard from, she had done something uncharacteristic: she had become a member of the National Organization for Women. She had mitigated the marriage imperative.

Sigmund Freud, the founder of psychoanalysis and a chief contributor to our present "mental health" imperatives, not only was sanguine about marriage as a salutary state of being but held that it was a necessary developmental stage, even an end-point of growth and maturation. Marriage, in Freud's vision, was a woman's overriding achievement.

Therefore, according to this psychology, if a woman after marriage became disturbed, it was because of deep emotional inadequacies and conflicts within her stemming from unresolved feelings of the childhood "family romance." He described the case of a woman who became severely psychotic directly after marriage in an essay entitled "Those Wrecked by Success"—the success here being that she achieved marriage: "People occasionally fall ill precisely when a deeply-rooted and long-cherished wish has come to fulfillment. It seems as though they were unable to tolerate their happiness; for there can be no question that there is a causal connection between their success and their falling ill."*

Freud then told of a "tragic" occurrence: A young woman "of good birth and well brought up . . . could not restrain her zest for life; she ran away from home and roamed about the world in search of adventure, until she made the acquaintance of an artist who could appreciate her feminine charms. . . . He took her to live with him and she proved a faithful companion to him, and seemed only to need social rehabilitation to achieve complete happiness. After many years of life together, he succeeded in getting his heretofore disapproving family reconciled to her and was prepared to make her his legal wife. She had never sought this status, never brought the issue to the fore and, alas, strangely (to him) showed no enthusiasm for it. He interpreted her paradoxical response as one of: 'it's too good to be true, or I can't believe something wonderful like this is really happening to me!'"

He pressed on with his determination toward the final act of rehabilitation, marriage. At this point, according to Freud, "she began to go to pieces. . . . She neglected the house of which she was now about to become the rightful mistress, imagined herself persecuted by his relations, who wanted to take her into the family, debarred her lover, through her senseless jealousy, from all social intercourse, hindered him in his artistic work, and soon succumbed to an incurable mental illness."

Freud's description of this case clearly reveals what may certainly be deemed his own bias about the marital state as well as what success is for every woman.

For Freud there is no question that marriage is this woman's success. She could harbor no other desire than to become

* Sigmund Freud, "Those Wrecked by Success," *On the History of the Psycho-Analytic Movement, Standard Edition*, vol. XIV, ed. and trans. James Strachey (New York: W. W. Norton, 1966), p. 317.

the artist's "legal wife"; therefore, she was wrecked by having her dream come true, assuming, as Freud does, that every woman has as her only central ambition the desire to become someone's legal wife. Freud completely ignored the possibility that a woman "of good birth and well brought up" might have some valid reservations about assuming a role (of wife) that carries with it a thicket of obligatory assumptions and duties that, as many today know, promote inferiority and diminution for the woman. She was hardly in a position to verbalize such sentiment lest she appear ungrateful or unloving. Indeed, the nonlegal relationship did meet her needs and provided an avenue for freedom that she apparently cherished up to then, as demonstrated by the description of her prior "errant" behavior.

Sadly, it was beyond Freud's comprehension that this woman, rather than being wrecked by success, was undone by a persistent, condescending lover who would not be contented until he gained legal power and authority over her—in the guise, of course, of both honoring and rehabilitating her.

This case description and Freud's great certainty here, as a paradigm for mental health and developmental psychology, make the claims of modern feminists against Freud plausible. His attitude about marriage as a woman's only valid success, so universally and uncritically accepted in the "helping professions," may be a principal reason why there has not been an adequate understanding of its possible destructive pressure on women in leading to other "feminine" syndromes including agoraphobia.

If the family lacks democracy, there is one thing the home is supposed to be for women: safe. It turns out, however, that home has not been the safe place it promised to be. The most dangerous place for women is in their own homes. One cannot read a newspaper without realizing the dangers of the street, yet social scientists have known for years what the public resists: the greatest danger is from "loved ones," and others whom we know.

For example, a 1979 report of spouse abuse in Kentucky, released by the Kentucky Commission on Women, reported that 10 percent of the married women in Kentucky had been physically abused during the year. The study further found that only 2 percent of the women questioned said they had ever been assaulted outside their homes. "A wife is better off in a bar than in her home," said Dr. Richard J. Gelles, sociologist, who was consultant for the study.*

Marriage can be dangerous to a woman's health in every country of the world. According to a UPI report, at least once a day a young bride in New Delhi, India, is burned to death or forced to swallow poison by her mother-in-law because her dowry is judged insufficient. The twenty-four-year-old bride of an automotive parts dealer died from burns she suffered after she was ignited by her husband's mother, who was dissatisfied with the woman's wedding gifts. Her dowry had included a television set, furniture, kitchenware, and china, but did not include the expected motor scooter.**

Although statistics again and again prove otherwise, people generally feel safer in their homes with relatives and friends than on the streets with strangers. One has always been safer with the "perfect" stranger than with those with whom we share our beds. Seven percent of the country's 47 million wives, about 3.3 million women, and .6 percent of husbands, about 280,000 men (there is much evidence that men underreport domestic violence for a variety of reasons), are victims of physical violence during domestic disputes. Probably even more serious are the physical and sexual assaults against children, who are generally powerless to react or adequately defend themselves, which occur within the house. Two million "battered child" cases were reported in 1978. Parents kick, punch, and bite 1.7 million children a year, and attack over 45,000 with knives and guns; 2.3 million children wield a gun or knife against a sibling. Two thousand

* "Safer in Bar," *Syracuse Post-Standard*, UPI report, July 6, 1979.
** "Brides Face Death for Small Dowry," *Syracuse Post-Standard*, July 10, 1979.

children will die of battering and at least 14,000 will suffer permanent brain damage.*

The agoraphobic who stays indoors to avoid dangers to life and limb is operating under a mythical assumption. This was emphasized by British psychiatrist Anthony Storr at a conference on family law. He defined the family, which is universally romanticized, as "the most violent institution in the world. It is our nearest and dearest who are most notably capable of provoking our intensest rage."**

* *Medical Tribune,* April 12, 1978.
** *Psychiatric News,* November 18, 1977.

2

Shopping: This Little Piggy Went to Market, This Little Piggy Stayed Home

> . . . the main thing today is—shopping. Years ago a person, he was unhappy, didn't know what to do with himself—he'd go to church, start a revolution—*something*. Today you're unhappy, can't figure it out? What is salvation? Go shopping.
>
> *Arthur Miller, The Price*

Sarah came for help in a state of desperation. Her marriage was in jeopardy and she felt she was a terrible mother. She was nearly completely housebound, unable to fulfill those tasks that wives and mothers are expected to perform. Principally, she was unable to do any of the shopping; that task now fell to her husband who was becoming disgruntled by this menial duty. Similarly, she lamented that she could not give her child the experience and excitement of trips to the stores and malls like the other mothers on the block. Sarah was ashamed of her seeming cowardice. But entering a store was impossible for her.

It all started shortly after her daughter was born. While shopping for groceries in the local supermarket, she experienced a spell of dizziness and she fainted. She was rushed by ambulance to a nearby hospital but regained consciousness by the time she arrived at the emergency room. Her physician was called and ordered her hospitalized. A thorough physical examination and a battery of tests disclosed nothing organically wrong. She was discharged and sent home.

Following this episode, Sarah found that fear of fainting again made her unable to enter stores or buildings, although she was able to leave the house for other purposes. No amount of cajoling, suggestion, or even threats could persuade her to enter a store. Tranquilizers, including antidepressants prescribed by her physician, were to no avail.

She made a series of accommodations. Friends and neighbors as well as a beleaguered husband filled in with shopping chores. She made arrangements with a local dress shop to send apparel to the house for selection. She purchased many items by mail from catalogues. All of these were a source of embarrassment. She was unable to do what any simple-minded person could do without effort or second thought.

Sarah's condition was an enigma to her. Reassured by specialists that there was nothing physically wrong with her, she remained terrified by the prospect of shopping. And where in the whole world, she reflected, are women more welcome and accepted than in stores?

After three years of suffering Sarah finally sought psychiatric help. She told her therapist that she was happily married and deeply in love with her husband. He was most attentive to her needs, even now in the years of inordinate stress due to her "illness." This made her feel even more inadequate and ungrateful.

Their marriage was a storybook success—romantic in essence and heartily approved of by both families. The birth of their child was planned and they were blessed with a beautiful and healthy daughter whom they both loved.

Her illness was a dark, threatening cloud in Camelot; she indeed had to be crazy to place all of this in jeopardy. Therefore, this errant behavior could not be of her doing but must be the manifestation of some morbid affliction, some medical imbalance, some dietary deficiency too obscure to be yet known to the medical profession. Her fainting spell had never been adequately explained. Some specialists hinted at epilepsy, which often acts capriciously and might recur at untoward times. Or, it might be a heart condition too slight or obscure to be detected by the means at hand.

She did reflect, however, that her fear of shopping was paradoxical since her jobs prior to marriage had entailed work in stores. She had been an account executive with an advertising agency; in the course of her work she checked on displays and often did product surveys in large malls and shopping centers. She made excellent progress in her work and was promoted ahead of schedule.

At the agency Sarah met and fell in love with Fred. After living together for about a year they felt they should marry. Fred was in his early thirties, already a vice-president, intent on starting a family. Sarah was hesitant because things were going so well, but she understandably could not reasonably discourage her lover's desire for a more stable arrangement.

They were married. Sarah quit her job; her salary was not needed and actually placed them in an untenable tax bracket. Instead she awaited a child and planned to devote herself to motherhood. She could always return to her career later.

So stores and public places were in no way alien to her. Additionally, as fate would have it, she came from a family of retailers. Her grandfather had built a chain of dry-goods stores across the nation. (What a field day for psychoanalysts here: Grandfather fills the country with stores; granddaughter can't shop.) Besides bringing wealth to the family, the chain provided managerial jobs for his sons and grandsons. As is the general custom, the women of the family were given stocks and bonds but never included in the management of the business. Sarah's father became part of this legacy but performed only marginally. He was the failure of the family.

Sarah's early life was filled with stories of business deals, new store openings and closings, bankruptcies and takeovers. She was intrigued by these machinations while at the same time knowing that she would never have an active role here. Her older brother entered the business immediately after college. She took this in good grace, started in her own chosen field, and began to make her mark.

What Sarah could never disclose—even to herself—was that from early childhood, despite a sterotypical female rearing, she had harbored ambitions to be part of the world of business and commerce and to be an heir to her grandfather's dynamism more than to the dynasty. She longed to be an active participant with a managerial role as was bestowed on even the least of the male members of the family. That of course was not to be (there are no affirmative action programs in family dynasties).

Sarah grew up in a home of constant family quarrels. Her mother's only refuge from the verbal conflicts with her husband was to take to her bed. She complained of severe headaches and she required sudden house calls from her physician. Frequently a nurse would have to attend to her. There were also the sedatives and sleeping pills, which on more than one occasion led to trips to emergency rooms.

Sarah's mother had grown up in a rural area of the South. She had been a beautiful adolescent and was state beauty queen at the age of eighteen. She was duly celebrated and exploited as is usually the fate of such teenagers. After her reign she aspired to a career on stage or modeling; she had understandably become infected with the public limelight.

However, the rich man's son met her and wooed her. After four months they were married and she settled down to be his wife. Even though she did not fulfull her aspirations for personal fame, she did pretty well by elevating herself from the poverty she had known as a child.

The marriage was turbulent from the outset. Besides differences in ethnicity, education, and religion, their behavior was that of two spoiled children out to destroy each other. He was a ne'er-do-well son who daily faced his apparent failures in the business world. All this he took out on his wife. For her part, she was not innocent; she had an inordinate appetite for accumulation and spent most of her nonsick time shopping and at the beauty parlor. This would set him off into fits of rage; he would accuse her of trying to bankrupt him and force him to crawl to his father and brothers to bail him out. This was almost a yearly occurrence despite his ample trust funds. But she couldn't quench her thirst for shopping and the bills continued to pile up. The marriage endured as if by fatal attraction. Two children were raised in these circumstances as witnesses and victims.

Sarah's main goal in life, as we would expect, was to be nothing like her mother and to marry a man who was in no way like her father. With irony she did just that. She married an ambitious and successful man whom she allowed to eclipse her. She herself became nonthreatening, outwardly weak, and nondemanding. She even became a nonshopper.

It was apparent that Sarah could not use her mother as a role model; that sort of dependent existence held no appeal. Yet as an emerging person she was not encouraged to develop her own talents nor was she given the opportunities automatically proffered to the men. And of course she wanted to remain "feminine" as was expected of the women in the family if they were to derive any benefits or gifts from the patriarch. This contributed to her dilemma. She was supposed to be content in being overlooked and dutifully looked over as her foremothers had been.

Sarah's marriage was a continuation of the self-abnegation and renunciation that she had experienced in her family, a painful repetition of being cavalierly dealt with by the caring and protective men in her life. Apparently it became too much; it went beyond the ultimate tolerance level and she would no longer cooperate. Among other vitally important grievances, she would not be reduced to what should be her glory-role—shopper.

One of the first symptoms of agoraphobia is a woman's inability to shop; panic attacks are experienced in supermarkets and in department stores. Needless to say, when a housewife cannot do the shopping, family arrangements change drastically. It might be observed that the housewife who is "too sick" to do the shopping is now spared a task that takes many hours of her week. But she pays a price: Even loving, indulgent husbands and children grow angry and irritated. Her children resent her behavior; her husband feels that their bargain has been broken.

Shopping is one of the principal occupations of wives. Women have been designated as the shoppers for all the small items that keep a household going. But in the real market, for example the stock market, where large transactions are made, the customers (not called shoppers now) are men, served mainly by other men. This shopping area is a male bastion;

because of the dimensions of the transactions involved, women are largely excluded.

If a woman voiced her apprehension on approaching Wall Street, no therapist would take her case. She would simply be told that she has no business being there in the first place. Serious concern from a therapist is elicited when her panic is related to visiting Macy's, Gimbel's, or Altman's—and the cure entails being able to shop in those places once again.

But the market may have hidden significance for a woman in a phylogenetic Jungian sense. Historically, and as still practiced openly in some parts of the world, women themselves have been on the block—bought, sold, traded, and bartered as commodities. The market is not an innocent area for her even though she will make no conscious connection between her now irrational phobia and the thousands of years that she herself was handled as a commodity. And one of the warnings that parents have habitually given daughters, even in sophisticated areas of the world, is the danger of being whisked away on the street, drugged, and sold into white slavery. Perhaps women have good and ample reasons for feeling uncomfortable in markets.

A multitude of wives have to depend on husbands as their sole means of support. Spending a lifetime being the recipient of another's generosity is demeaning and precarious: Even the kindest and most open-handed donor can question and demand a reckoning, and can exercise the power of withdrawal or denial. Even if never exercised, the power in reserve is there to make the other feel guilty and ultimately to terrorize. Through the years in the course of these transactions, wives have responded to their personal dependence and poverty by developing a system of lying, cheating, and stealing (from husbands and other family members), using their principal vocation, shopping.

Deception about the cost of things is the most useful ploy (now on the decrease because more women are working outside the home and earning their own money). A woman without her own money can tell her husband she bought a new dress on sale for $60, although she paid $150 for it, using funds she saved from her food allowance. Her husband will be pleased with the bargain: His wife will be well-dressed, contributing to his status in the community; his wife, he thinks, spends less money than his friends' wives to present an elegant appearance. He has the best of both worlds—a wife who spends money with care but looks like a million dollars.

Because husbands themselves eat, they are somewhat more accepting of dubious food bills. But the matter of the bargain is the important issue. The wife must show that she can strike a good bargain and that she is constantly on the lookout for one. Bargain psychology is an integral part of the marital relationship. Ultimately the wife must portray herself as being a bargain, costing less and doing better at the *agora* than the other wives, other women to whom he could be married. Being a bargain, however, becomes part of a self-cheapening process leading to pejoration of the human spirit. It costs a great deal in the end.

Other tricks in the wife's underground economy are developed to convert things into cash. Many men who are unswerving devotees of capitalism often don't trust their own wives with money. The economic situation of most women with wealthy husbands is that they themselves have little access to cash. Women as a class are perennial recipients, a status male children grow out of or relinquish.

Why do women steal from stores? The answer must be that they have no other place to steal from. By definition, there is no kleptomania among the poor; they are said to lift or steal. No fancy, "treatable" condition for them. Kleptomania is a term applied mainly to the well-to-do women who take from counters when there is no visible need. They can easily afford to buy what they want, yet still they place themselves in seemingly unnecessary and irrational jeopardy.

Women who otherwise could buy the items they steal are called neurotic. But these women often feel more honorable stealing than chronically being a recipient of another's generosity. And to assume that women are immune from larcenous instincts is part of the Madonna image that men have imposed on women. When women steal it is classified as a perversion. It is surely perverse for affluent men or their women to stoop to theft the way poor people do. One must stick to the methods of one's social and economic class. It must be some form of insanity to risk the penalties and public humiliation that comes from ordinary shoplifting.

Women are the kleptomaniacs first of all because despite the image of the wealthy wife of the wealthy man, most "rich" women are not rich at all. Law students are taught in their first course in wills and trusts that "the purpose of the laws on estates is to keep money out of the hands of women." Rich women, even rich widows, usually do not have access to money. It is controlled by male bankers, male accountants, male attorneys, and often, their own sons.

Second, women are the kleptomaniacs because the stores are their arena. Shopping is the occupation of women. The inability to go into stores is considered a sign of disease in women. Many a healthy man has never set foot in a supermarket, yet a woman who cannot enter a supermarket is diagnosed as sick.

If a man has larcenous intent, he can manipulate the silver market, he can juggle the books, he can raise the price of gasoline. If a woman is going to steal, she can do it only in the arena where she lives. So she contracts a woman's disease and works her larceny in her place of activity.

People of all economic classes have in common the propensity for humiliating those they love. Therefore, women have converted shopping and its tricks—the one public freedom given to them—to a means of participating in the capitalist system. Many of these struggles for cash are enormously time-consuming: well-dressed wives on the street selling gasoline purchased with credit cards; international socialites selling designer dresses to their neighbors to get cash; a group of friends choosing a restaurant for luncheon on the basis of which establishment honors the credit card that the woman who needs cash is carrying.

It is not uncommon for children to steal money from their mothers' purses. Just as common is the mother who is reduced to stealing money from her child's allowance. Fathers are often more generous to their children than to their wives.

However, shopping is the principal medium through which a wife can work her economic deceptions. It is in this area that she has some residual power of staying even, and, alas, of getting even. Along with advances in trading technology, charge accounts, credit cards, and automatic loans, her own skills have escalated, talents that generate no pride in self and set no good example for her children. Her valuable energies are here perverted and wasted.

With the onset of agoraphobia, suddenly and without explanation there is a panic reaction and shopping ceases. Just as men generally abhor routine shopping and consider it to be women's work, so too some women begin to feel they have had enough of the diminution they experience as perennial shoppers.

The most prevalent mode of "treatment" for agoraphobia is a visit to a department store: This is not only a reward for good behavior, but evidence of the "cure." Emergence out of the house and into the world is not celebrated by a trip to a library or a museum, to the university or the courthouse; it is a trip to Bloomingdale's or Macy's, where the woman can resume her work as the family shopper.*

---

* New video technology including two-way communication between home and stores may turn agoraphobia into a virtue. "Videotex" may put the behaviorists out of business. See Eric Pace, "System Will Permit Shopping at Home, *New York Times* Business Section, April 14, 1982.

3

The Work Strike

Behind the layers of ambiguity and dissonance the agoraphobic longs for meaningful and rewarding involvement in the outside world. This may mean that there were lapses and breaches in her early feminine training that make it difficult for her to accept the renunciations usually demanded of women.

It is then a trivialization of her humanity to explain away her condition and behavior as merely a learning failure or a fear of fear as many have done, thereby justifying simpleminded remedies that may in fact go contrary to the agoraphobic's hidden and unspoken goals.

When a housewife declares that she can no longer leave home to do the shopping, to drive the children to their activities, to accompany her husband on obligatory social and/or professional events, how can we not wonder if there is some minimal strike involved against these housewife expectations, despite all her protestations of desire and willingness? At the same time, can we not suspect her of implementing this strike with a caricature of the feminine sex role? Without perhaps fully comprehending the validity of the protest motivation, observers have noted that hysteria in women displays this caricature of femininity. A woman who appears completely housebound—the literal "housewife"—achieves such a caricature. And synchronous with the purpose of caricature in general she too hopes to get a message across: "Woman's place is in the home."*

The work action used by certain essential government employees comes to mind. Air traffic controllers, people deemed almost indispensable to our well-being, are forbidden to strike. Instead they resort to a work caricature that frustrates the operations of the airports yet seemingly does not violate the law against striking. Their tactics are largely successful. They operate strictly by the rules; they go by the book, refusing to allow the elasticity or margin of movement that realistically must be exercised in the day-to-day operation of air traffic. The effect of this literal behavior is to bring almost all airport operations to a halt.

Other public employees similarly prohibited from striking feign illness. Firefighters and the police often have sick-outs, their illnesses validated by notes from sympathetic physicians. It is difficult to argue with confirmed illness even when the illness strikes suddenly and massively and disappears when conditions and grievances are met. Never, however, do those stricken admit to any ruse or strategy.

An interesting parallel is how reassured many agoraphobics are when they are diagnosed as suffering from a real disease. In the same vein, it may help to explain why they so readily submit to dubiously effective medical and related procedures to cure their affliction. Although it is acceptable (and cynically expected) for women to be ill, not so if their defection from work is ideologically motivated.

In the helping professions, as is shown later, the emphasis is so overwhelming on the clinical aspects of this condition that the woman as a reacting, striving human being becomes obscured. Ironically, this misplaced emphasis at some point

* Paul Chodoff and Henry Lyons, "Hysteria, The Hysterical Personality and 'Hysterical' Conversion," *American Journal of Psychiatry* 114, 8 (February 1958): 734–40. See also Carroll Smith-Rosenberg, "The Hysterical Woman: Sex Roles Conflict in 19th Century America," *Social Research* 39 (1972): 652–78; Paul Chodoff, "Hysteria and Woman," *American Journal of Psychiatry* 139 (May 1982): 545–55.

may play the same role as the sympathetic physicians with their public employee patients in the sickout.

In October 1978 *The Wall Street Journal* reported on a strike in Nancy, France. Two hundred women workers had locked themselves inside a factory in order to retain their jobs, now in jeopardy because of the bankruptcy of the family-owned clothing business, Entreprise Glotz.

The factory looks abandoned; the front gates are chained and locked, telephones have been disconnected. But there is life inside—an occupation force of women have prevented the banks from taking possession of the premises.

The strikers say they seek to assure themselves jobs when they find a new patron or boss to manage the business more successfully. Strange behavior to an American observer; apparently in France this is how the labor movement works.

The *Journal* suggests that the women at the Glotz factory "seem unlikely to win any medals for a long strike." For one thing, none of their dozen male ex-colleagues is supporting the takeover; many husbands have persuaded their wives to stay away. Yet although a few policemen could easily open the gates, the government is loath to provoke controversy by ousting the women.

The general nonsupport of the women is interpreted as "Gallic male chauvinism" since French women are expected to remain in the home, not on the barricades. These women might be suffering from an affliction the opposite of agoraphobia, reluctance to leave the marketplace for their homes. They know that their destinies are at the factory. They say: "To occupy a factory is to refuse to be unemployed." A strike leader declares: "They couldn't find any other jobs, even if there were some." Some of the women strikers have worked at Glotz for forty-three years.

Here is a serious job action indeed, a protest against being undone, having their lives sabotaged. Is the agoraphobic who won't leave her home enacting a one-person lock-in—yet unwilling or unable to articulate accumulated grievances, in its own way a life-saving device? And is forcing her out before assurances are given or demands met a form of strike-breaking? Is it simply an issue of bad education for which she is to be retrained, as the behaviorists would have us believe? Surely no one would consider the French women's occupation of the factory and the reluctance to leave as simply stubborn or irrational fearfulness. Yet the French women might very well display extreme emotional and physical reactions to any efforts forcing them to evacuate their position. These reactions, any sensitive observer would agree, are not due to physical, endocrinal, or psychopathological disorders.

The labor movement in general has interesting metaphors for the woman's homebound role in our culture. One of the great weaknesses for women in the labor movement is that as women slowly began to enter the work force they tended to join unions less often than men. Women also tended to form separate unions. The primary reason is tediously obvious: The men did not want them.

A second reason is that women who work outside the home also have jobs inside their homes, which gives them different, tighter schedules. A spokeswoman to a garment worker's local in 1908 reported: "The reason why the women had to draw out from the men was because the men wanted to come late to the meetings and stay late while the women wanted to go early and come home early."*

Women workers also complained that men monopolized the meetings and that they could not speak when men were present. Not being able to speak when men are present, not being able to express their oppression or otherwise protest the secondary role in the world that they have been expected and forced to assume as part of their femininity, helps explain the use of such strategies as hysteria with its obstinancies and exaggerations.

The agoraphobic woman is actually abiding strictly by the rules of the game. She has learned the historical lesson and like the air traffic controllers she is going by the book, much to the consternation of all concerned. We perceive agoraphobia

---

* National Women's Trade Union League, *Proceedings of the 1908 Interstate Conference*, pp. 19–20.

as a very personalized sit-in strike, a metaphor of bold definition. If woman's place is indeed in the home, she will be
there—with a vengeance. If being dependent and living vicar-
iously is woman's lot in life, who is more womanly and feminine than the agoraphobe? But alas, as everyone knows, there
is method in conformity, sometimes more than in madness.

In the mid-fifties, the wife of a politician appeared for treatment of phobias that prevented her from performing her
wifely duties, in this case accompanying her husband during
his campaigns in addition to the household tasks. At first she
was always at his side, but when he ran for reelection she
noticed that she was becoming increasingly incapacitated,
with no apparent reason. As he spoke or mingled with func-
tionaries or constituents, she became lightheaded and over-
whelmed by the feeling that she would "pass out." At first
they thought the hot smoke-filled rooms or the crowds press-
ing in on her were having a psychological effect, but all types
of reassurance and accommodations proved to no avail. Yet
this task was expected of her; he had to appear with a loving,
caring, and supporting family, especially as there had been
"rumors" about him.

In order to brace herself, she started to drink, which
seemed to help. But the amount had to be progressively increased. There was also embarrassment when people noticed
her condition. Finally she had to be left behind, much to the
chagrin of political managers, her husband, and all the rest of
her family. She had let everyone down; her own parents
scolded her for her disgusting and contemptible behavior. In
presenting herself for help, she explained that she just had to
get over this "sickness" that was damaging her husband's career and would certainly wreck her marriage and household.
She insisted that the only thing in this world that she wanted
was to be able to help her husband and make him proud of
her. Failing this, she felt her life would be a complete defeat.

Yet she seemed helpless in overcoming her difficulties.
Her home remedies as well as the sedatives given by her
doctor only compounded the problem. She would repeat,
"John deserves better. He has worked so very hard to get

where he is. He certainly does not need an albatross around his neck." Her rhetoric (and perhaps "illness") was typical of her calamitous decade. For in the fifties a wife, especially a political wife, was there to be helpful in all things, to be altruistic, always living with derived happiness.

Derived happiness has not been successful for a wide variety of women of varied backgrounds. There is the case of Supreme Court Justice Felix Frankfurter and his wife, Marion. There has been speculation about the unsuccessful aspects of the Frankfurter marriage, including Marion Frankfurter's psychiatric problems. She was the daughter of a Congregational minister of old Yankee stock. She married an immigrant Jew and was therefore purportedly subjected to unaccustomed social pressures. Also it was said by some that she was too frail to cope adequately with Frankfurter's dynamic and aggressive personality.

Her husband's diaries, however, suggest another cause of her difficulties.* Before her marriage, Marion Frankfurter was Phi Beta Kappa at Smith College and president of the student body. She also did graduate work at Smith in economics. She was a militant proponent of women's suffrage, worked at the New York School for Social Work, enlisted in the War Camp Activities Bureau, and during the war worked in France with the Red Cross.

Her husband had a different view of the ideal woman. For example, he praised one woman as "a splendid type . . . whose essential career is through her husband." He wrote: "How deeply women sink themselves in others—someone must be the object of their devotion."** The diaries make several references to important conversations that took place after dinner, "when the men were alone." Once even Frances Perkins, then secretary of labor, was excluded.

It is not unlikely that the anguish of Marion Frankfurter had more to do with attempting to sink herself into others, Phi

---

* Joseph P. Lash, *From the Diaries of Felix Frankfurter* (New York: W. W. Norton, 1975), pp. 30, 31, 39, 88.
** Ibid., pp. 102, 109.

Beta Kappa notwithstanding, than with the difficulties of a Yankee's adapting to immigrant Jewish ways.

Contrast this with Dr. Ernestine Schlant, the wife of Senator Bill Bradley. She is a person with a strong identity, earned from her own efforts, who finds herself the wife of a famous basketball star turned politician. Although she was not asked, she felt obliged to help him in his campaign. "Dr. Schlant said her husband did not pressure her to campaign for him last fall and left it totally up to her what she would contribute to his campaign. Dr. Schlant said she preferred to campaign separately from her husband 'because I felt I didn't want to stand in Bill's shadow and stretch out my hand and say, "Here is the wife." ' " *

In 1958 there existed neither the understanding that wives have needs and desires apart from husbands nor the acceptable rhetoric to make a case for themselves—only "body language" was available. Twenty years later it is possible for a politician's wife, even while being helpful and supportive, to write her own ticket. Certainly living in another's shadow was just as onerous in the fifties as now, but there was no rhetoric for saying so. Living in the shadow of a great man was supposed to be an honor.

There is little chance that Ernestine Schlant will be a candidate for agoraphobia. She will not conform to the usual role of a wife of a U.S. Senator: "a helpmate to her husband, his social chairman and confidante, the uncomplaining mother of his children and, if she had any spare time, the volunteer bandage-roller with the other Senate wives."** Instead she will spend her time researching her new book, *An Inquiry Into the Historical Consciousness of 20th-Century German Writers*. And instead of following the biblical Ruth's imperative, she and her husband will alternate commuting on weekends between Washington and their home in New Jersey.

Throughout our country's history the definition of woman's proper place has been inconsistent. However, domestic obli-

---

* Judy Klemesrud, *The New York Times*, December 29, 1978, p. A15.
** Ibid.

gations have always been considered an absolute. Even where a woman is allowed, even expected, to pursue meaningful and well-paying employment (such as in today's educated middle class), domestic obligations have not changed. Even the wealthy woman is still expected to oversee her (mostly female) household staff.

In most living situations, it is the woman who either cares for the child or provides for child care, who either shops and cooks or arranges for someone else to do it, who either cleans the home or provides for a substitute person to provide this service. Even more significant than the division of domestic chores within the home is the perception of the wife's legitimate functions outside the home. A proper wife attends to only those activities outside the home that enhance her husband and his interests: his career, his children, his dwelling.

A woman is mentally disturbed who is unable to leave the house to purchase groceries, attend her husband's corporation banquet, or drive the children to Little League. A woman who is unable to leave the house to attend a NOW meeting, to return to graduate school, or to visit an art exhibit is not considered similarly ill.

So attuned must a wife be to her husband's needs that women who earn substantial salaries are often asked if their husbands mind the size of their incomes. She is supposed to worry about his bruised ego, which would have to be weak indeed to overshadow the desire of most people to have more money in these inflation-ridden times. Husbands who earn more money than their wives are not asked if their wives mind—it is assumed they like it.

In the 1880s childrearing manuals gave primacy to maternal instincts and the innate and all-beneficial effect of motherly affection. By the 1920s mother love was under suspicion as a possible means of smothering a child. A new definition of proper womanhood emerged, one which in no way would free women from some necessary tasks, but imposed a more complicated one. "Educated motherhood" focused on the needs of the child and the need to educate and train women so they could attend to child development. Instinct was no longer enough. As Sheila Rothman observed: "The 1920's witnessed . . . the rise of the concept of woman as 'wife-companion.' It was a romantic and sexual definition, moving women from the nursery to the bedroom even as it kept them at home."*

Although our early universities did not admit women, women's colleges eventually emerged, as did co-educational institutions. The problem of how to keep women satisfied with home life after they had received higher education was thoroughly dealt with. Catharine Beecher, writer of advice books for women, urged women "to obtain appropriate scientific and practical training for their distinctive profession as housekeeper, nurse of infants and the sick, educator of childhood, trainer of servants and minister of charities."

One of the tasks of women in the 1880s was to curb their husbands' animal instincts. "Few women understand at the outset, that in marrying, they have simply captured a wild animal . . . the taming of which is to be the life work of the woman who has taken him in charge. . . . The duty is imposed upon her by high heaven, to reduce all these grand, untamed life-forces in order . . . to make them subservient to the behests of her nature, and to those vast undying interests which, to these two and to their posterity, center in the home."**

Medical authorities reinforced the idea of woman's proper place. Physicians insisted that biological characteristics permitted women to pursue only certain activities. Woman's very refinement and moral sensibility were the root causes of the prevailing female maladies, they said. These maladies made active participation in the world outside the home dangerous if not impossible. "It was as if the Almighty, in creating the female sex, had taken the uterus and built up a woman around

* *Woman's Proper Place: A History of Changing Ideals and Practices, 1870 to the Present* (New York: Basic Books, 1980), pp. 5–6.
** John S. Haller and Robin M. Haller, *The Physician and Sexuality in Victorian America* (Champaign: University of Illinois Press, 1974), p. 90.

it."* According to *Transactions* in 1875: "Woman has a sum total of nervous force equivalent to a man's, but this force is distributed over a greater multiplicity of organs. . . . The nervous force is therefore weakened in each organ . . . it is more sensitive, more liable to derangement."

The onset of menstruation supposedly increased this debilitation, and girls were instructed to limit their physical and intellectual activities during this time. The notion that menstruation makes a difference in female capacity is alive and well today. In both the Soviet Union and the People's Republic of China, women are excused from work during this time. In China it is believed that allowing women to enter the rice fields while they are menstruating endangers the crops. In the Soviet Union, time off for menstruation is written into the labor laws.

A guide to married life published in 1901 advises that "Long walks are to be avoided. Also long wheel rides . . . in fact, all severe physical exertion. . . . Intense mental excitement as a fit of anger or grief or even intense joy may be injurious." The marriage guide also warned about the dangers to the mother and her baby if these rules were disregarded. "Many a young wife has died in childbirth because of the uterine ailments contracted in girlhood through improper dress or injudicious conduct." The contemporary legal decisions reflected the medical concern for keeping woman in the home and off her feet. Case after case was resolved by stating that the woman's place was in the home—not in the jury box, not in the workplace, not at the ballot box. All these judges used as a rationale the medical data available to them, data written by male doctors about their female patients.

Since women menstruate during a great part of their lives, they could effectively be kept out of public life by a declaration that disobeying medical orders about their own frailty could endanger the next generation. A woman who disre-

* Quoted in Charles E. Rosenberg and Carroll Smith-Rosenberg, "The Female Animal: Medical and Biological Views of Women in Nineteenth-Century America," *Journal of American History* 60 (September 1973): 56.

garded her doctor's orders was not only suicidal, she was dooming the race.

Women were cautioned to avoid enervating situations not only because of their internal organs, but because they were predisposed to neurasthenia. Hysteria could erupt at any time. Isaac Ray, a leading psychiatrist of the time, wrote "with women it is but a step from extreme nervous susceptibility to downright hysteria and from that to overt insanity. In the sexual evolution, in pregnancy, in the parturient period, in lactation, strange thoughts, extraordinary feelings, unreasonable appetites, criminal impulses may haunt a mind at other times innocent and pure."*

The American Medical Association counseled that "women in a few exceptional cases may have all the courage, tact, ability, pecuniary means, education and patience necessary to fit persons for the cares and responsibilities of professional life, but they still are and must be subject to the periodical *infirmity* of their sex; which for the time and in every case, *however unattended by physical suffering,* unfits them for any responsible effort of mind, and in many cases of body also." At the turn of the century the medical profession was taught that even if a woman has no symptoms of unfitness, she is unfit anyway.

As Sheila Rothman explains, the women's colleges established in the post–Civil War period represented both an acknowledgment of societal assumptions about the peculiarities of the female sex and a novel response to them. When Matthew Vassar opened his college for women in 1865, it provided women not only with an opportunity for education but also with ways of overcoming their seeming predispositions to illness.

The trustees were bombarded by the judgments of male doctors warning that "the physical organization and function of woman naturally disqualify her for severe study, and that an

---

* Quoted in G. J. Barker-Benfield, *The Horrors of the Half-Known Life* (New York: Harper & Row, 1976), p. 83.

education essentially popular and largely ornamental is alone suited to her sphere."*

Women had been admitted to Oberlin in 1834 but they were not routinely allowed into the courses open to men. If they first proved themselves in the Ladies Course, they were later admitted into other courses. The women who argued for a more intense education did not refute the idea that a woman's place was in the home, not in college and the library. They argued that educated women would make better wives and mothers.

At the turn of the century many young women were away from home working in factories and earning their own money. But just as the college students were told that studying too much would injure their brains and their reproductive capacities, female factory workers were encouraged to take employment in the home, anybody's home. Reformers visited them at factories, telling them that factory employment was demoralizing to young women. One philanthropic representative wrote, in an attempt to steer women from factories, "The farther the woman drifts from the family and the home, the more she is in danger from the shoals and quicksands of society."

* John H. Raymond, *Vassar College: Its Foundation, Aims, Resources and Course of Study*, 1873, p. 21.

4

The Psychology of Outside and Inside

Before I built a wall I'd ask to know what I was walling
in or walling out.

"Mending Wall"
Robert Frost

Agoraphobia lends itself to fascinating speculation as to
etiology and origins. Is the condition in its most primitive
ontological dimension a reliving of the birth trauma itself, the
exit from the warm, secure, enclosed womb into the unen-
closed, structureless chaos of the extrauterine world?

It was Otto Rank's view that the trauma of birth, the memory of our genesis, is the archetype of all the fears of change, of
loss, of movement, the primordial insecurity that all living
beings carry with them as part of their biological and social
history. This is a memory that we are not apt to forget: Its
effects on our life and destiny have to be great. But it is un-
clear and unknown, as Freud was to point out, just how much
a memory it could be, given the incomplete development of
the nervous system at the time of birth. There are many who
place great stock in precognitive memories, who make claims
for intrauterine memories. The warm, enclosed home, in contrast to the cold, alien, hostile out-of-doors does lend itself to
unmistakable womb imagery. The housebound woman cannot
escape the accusation of clinging to comforts from which all
must leave.

There are a number of events of infancy and childhood that
intensify and augment the safety of the inside and the fear of
the outside. Foremost is the pleasure and security of being

embraced by parent or nurse, as opposed to being left alone in a crib. The routine practice of swathing in many European countries tries to recreate the protective warmth of an enclosure. And the crib itself is often designed to emulate an eggshell. Similarly, good infant care practices dictate that in feeding, breast or otherwise, the child be held close to the body of the nurturing person. As recognition evolves in the neonate, he or she begins to perceive that the comfort and reassurance of the caring people seem to disappear as they leave the room for outer space, outer rooms, and the outside.

The grownups disappear into the great unknown, sometimes irretrievably gone. There is much in the background and social life of the infant that makes outer space threatening to the self-preservation of the organism. It is where the nurturing and comforting objects vanish. As cognition increases, it becomes apparent that the feeding, caring, familiar objects are inside, the strange untouching, nonfeeding persons on the outside. One could indeed freeze and starve out there on the porch.

After the experience of the mainly biological aspects of the outside-inside phenomenon, there are decisive developmental forces germane to agoraphobia that determine how the person perceives and experiences this dichotomy. Agoraphobia is primarily a woman's strategy; one might say it is second nature to her, because being on the inside is the programming she receives as the traditional and normal female upbringing. Being homebound is a major part of the process of becoming feminine.

In this interior setting she is taught the home arts of working, serving, and cleaning as well as the rehearsals for the role of mothering. She sees her mother or another woman (servant, sister, grandmother) doing these things. They define femininity for her.

Activities outside the home are by and large part of the masculine stereotype. Subtly or blatantly, the girl is impressed that the out-of-doors is a male preserve where she is unwelcome except at certain times and places. Similarly strongly enforced restrictions are placed on the distance from home she can wander or to whom she can speak.

Although some changes are being effected in breaking down these sex-role stereotypes, the overwhelming force of historical precedent, social custom, and prejudice still dominate in the rearing of children today, clearly to the female's disadvantage. This early severe deprivation must leave its mark on the developmental process and also on the degree of comfort and compatibility a woman can achieve in a basically hostile and alien outside world.

There are those who discount these inequities as unimportant, invoking the opposite-but-equal doctrine. Psychoanalysis, to its discredit, fostered an "anatomy is destiny" developmental psychology that gave little hope for improvement through social enlightenment and change. Its tenets are well known, based on male supremacy due not to choice or oppression but the unalterable realities of anatomy. The male has a penis that is prominent and visible from the time of birth; it is on the outside. In early childhood the female has nothing comparable to show. This must, we are told, shape her whole psychology, part of which must entail acceptance, if she is to be mentally healthy, of her own interiority cum inferiority. Even the enlightened Erik Erikson, in the forefront when it comes to perceiving the social oppression of blacks, Jews, and young people, fell back on anatomy to explain the plight of women. He designated early childhood as the period in which the vast differences (largely anatomical) between the destinies of the male and female child take place.

He described the differences: The boy has something to show, a wondrous piece of equipment, the penis. The young girl has nothing visible, not even budding breasts. She must turn inward for her ego sustenance. Whatever value she has must be on the inside, if anywhere. Erikson might have said "inside her skull," but that was not to be. Anatomy refers only to genitals in this developmental scheme. Her hopes and fears, indeed her destiny, are dependent on these organs. Erikson writes that the body image of the girl "includes a valuable inside, an inside on the development of which depends her fulfillment as an organism and as a role bearer. This fear of being left empty, and, more simply, that of being left, seems to be the most basic feminine fear, extending over the whole of a woman's existence. It is normally intensified with each menstruation and takes its final toll during the menopause. No wonder, then, that the anxiety aroused by these fears can express itself either in complete subjection to male thought, in desperate competition with it, or in efforts to catch the male and make him a mere tool."*

Erikson confirms that women are "bitches" because of anatomical misfortunes. Even their "neurotic fears" of being abandoned or otherwise left behind have no basis in social reality but can be explained by anatomy and physiology. Obviously social remedies would be futile. And "regrettably," men become their victims.

If being left really is woman's most basic fear, we don't have to seek its origins in anatomy. Women have been left behind in practically all areas of private and public affairs. They have been left behind in educational opportunities, wages, promotions, and challenges commensurate with ability. Typical of those making self-serving explanations, Erikson wants us to believe that woman's fear of being left is neurotic, due to her internal genital spaces that have to be filled. He overlooks the social reality that fathers, husbands, brothers, and sons are programmed and encouraged to leave "their" women behind.

To be empty, to be poor or powerless, is to be a servant. The woman supposedly escapes the feelings of servitude and inferiority by filling herself and the household. It is understandable that she must later suffer the "empty nest syndrome" as husband and children leave. We see that for her all is biological; little is said about filling her cranium or coffers, which, of course, are the male prerogative.

In June 1976 Ann Landers wrote a shocking article for *Good Housekeeping*. She had asked her readers: "If you had it

---

* *Childhood and Society* (New York: W. W. Norton, 1950), p. 366.

to do over again—would you have children?" Ten thousand women answered. The so-called empty nest syndrome, assumed to be almost universal among women in their forties who have sent their youngest child off to college, turns out to be something else. To Landers's horror, 70 percent said that if they had known then what they know now, they would not have children.

Often the agoraphobic will extend her area of safety beyond the home itself. This might be to the town library and the path or street leading to it. Or it may be a family cottage on a lake to which she can be driven. Similarly, a particularly friendly neighbor's home may become a place where she does not experience anxiety or panic. The condition is variable and compromises can be made with the outside world, giving the agoraphobic more *Lebensraum*. This process is akin to annexations and conquests that increase the territory where a nation's citizens may live and roam comfortably. Perhaps there is an element of agoraphobia in empire-building "territorial imperatives."

Alien or hostile spaces can be domesticated for the agoraphobic if conditions, which only she knows, are met. From this process of selectivity there is the hope that more and more of the world may become safe and hospitable. In this selectivity, the agoraphobic may appear to be playing tricks. The impatient spouse or relative might say, "How come you can go to places you like, but never seem to be able to go to my places?"

Because of the rigid sex-role conditioning in early childhood and the messages given in adult exclusions, there is a bit of agoraphobia in all women thusly exposed. Not the full-blown clinical entity, it shows itself in various subtle habits and attitudes. There is the tether phenomenon. Some women immediately feel uncomfortable when driving more than a certain distance from their homes, say, beyond the shopping areas. A great many women will not attend meetings or courses after dark. Conversely there are women who feel comfortable only after dusk (when the world reverts to them from male daytime domination). Women are more apt to stay indoors during inclement weather (fear of falling, suffering personal injury or disease).

There are other subtle everyday indicators. A woman will say, "I ran out of money so I didn't leave the house all winter"; or the ubiquitous "I never leave home without my makeup on," "I didn't go because I didn't have anything to wear." How often we hear "I can't leave the house looking like a mess." These can be perceived as protective rituals.

Therefore, with strong developmental conditioning that belonging and performing in the home are an integral part of femininity, in addition to a generally perceived inimicality of the outside in terms of inordinate deprivation later in life, it is not difficult to understand why women become homebound either partially or completely.

Jews as a people have had to resort to various tricks of survival in dealing with a hard and unrelenting patriarchal diety, as well as an historically hostile world. They are known to give false identification data in order to fool the Angel of Death. They get around the tithing requirement by "boarding out" cattle to Christian neighbors. Similarly, outsiders are used to light the "Saturday" stove.

Orthodox Jews have a practice that is quite similar to the "annexations" of agoraphobics. A report describes an unbroken chain of fences, telephone wires, fish lines and wire going up around a section of northwest Baltimore. When it is finished, "Carol Miller will be able to take her children on the streets on Saturdays."*

Miller is one of five thousand Orthodox Jews living among a community of forty-one thousand people from a variety of ethnic groups. They are solving the problem of how to make life on the day of the Sabbath more comfortable for themselves and their children. Carrying objects, including children, on the street outside of the household is forbidden on the Sabbath. Originally this was a prohibition against outside work: The Sabbath should be a day of rest. This means, however,

---

* *Syracuse Post-Standard*, June 10, 1978.

that infants and small children, complete with paraphernalia, cannot be carried on the street. All must be housebound.

The Orthodox of Baltimore used their ingenuity to get around this inconvenience without "breaking the Law." They did this by expanding the idea of "household" (where carrying is permitted) to include the entire Orthodox Jewish neighborhood. The idea was concretized by mechanical measures that allowed the whole section to be fenced in without obstructing or interfering in the lives of their non-Orthodox neighbors. The fence is a symbol, not a barrier.

They constructed an inconspicuous, symbolic sixteen-mile wall (*eruv* in Hebrew) consisting of some new elements, but also using structures already in the environment. So, in addition to fish lines and wires, at intersections where fencing could not be erected telephone wires already strung across the street are considered a part of the wall.

To a strict constructionist this may appear to stretch things a bit too far, taking license as to what is a "household." One can say that the solution is a legalistic compromise by a group that is determined to preserve a tradition without enduring the hardship that might cause many to abandon the community altogether. A compromise is reached, a theological gerrymandering that gives the appearance of piety and at the same time pays heed to practical human needs. But a wall cannot be strictly imaginary. It must have props, as if to give external evidence to the Angel-Inspector-General that the Sabbath is indeed being properly observed.

It is not only the Orthodox Jews in Baltimore who must deal with the issue of walls and fences. In Pittsburgh, tightly knit communities of Slovaks, Poles, Croatians, and other Eastern Europeans remain remarkably intact. Homes are passed from generation to generation and few are for sale to outsiders. Catholic and Eastern Orthodox churches predominate in the community; fraternal organizations and social clubs, in addition to folk festivals and ethnic food stores, provide ties to the residents' past.

These enclaves have survived so well for so long in part due to Pittsburgh's geography—natural barriers help to pre-

serve neighborhoods intact.* Most Pittsburghers, according to
a poll, identify far more with their neighborhoods than with
the city as a whole. Some seldom venture beyond them; home
is the South Side or Polish Hill, not Pittsburgh.

In addition to physical barriers, the neighbors have stayed
together because of social forces. Many faced the contempt of
native-born Americans and immigrants who arrived earlier
than they did. Most in the neighborhoods can afford to move,
but cannot imagine doing so. Some third-generation Slavs, for
example, unable to find houses for sale in the old neighborhood, have actually built new homes in their parents' back-
yards.

We can all applaud the good sense of people who have not
moved miles from the city. But for these ethnic groups in
Pittsburgh, for the Orthodox Jews in Baltimore, as well as for
those who feel they do not wish to leave home at all for the
outside, we can respect their understanding, conscious or not,
that they are not totally welcome in the world beyond the
particular set of walls they have chosen to call their own.

---

* Carol Hymowitz, "Staying Home," *The Wall Street Journal*, September
12, 1979.

5

Emily Dickinson: A Woman Who Chose
to Stay at Home

Of Fate if this is All
Has he no added Realm
A Dungeon but a Kinsman is
Incarceration—Home.

Emily Dickinson

Emily Dickinson is probably the best-known recluse in
history. She was raised in an intellectual and political family
in Amherst, Massachusetts. Her father was a prominent and
well-respected attorney. She was highly educated, both at
home and at Mount Holyoke.

She spent her life writing poetry. She accumulated 1,775
poems in her room—trunks full. Her position in nineteenth-
century American letters is secure: She is one of the significant poets of that time, although opinions differ as to whether
she was revolutionary in her style and hence the creator of
new directions in poetry, or simply a superb romantic poet.

Dickinson died in 1886 at age fifty-five. For the last
twenty-five years of her life she did not leave her home. She
received visitors, but did not pay visits. Often she spoke to her
visitors while she stood in the hall and they remained in the
parlor.

Literary historians have speculated on her life and on her
seclusion. Much of her work deals with nature and with personal relationships, probably because these subjects were the
genre of poetry at that time, and also because personal rather
than political issues have been considered the province of
women (poets and nonpoets) for centuries.

Dickinson lived during one of the most turbulent periods
in history. Revolutions were fought all over Europe; the Civil

War tore the United States apart; American capitalism took root and began to flourish; eastern Americans began to move west; the natural resources of North America were noted as unprecedented in the world. All this must have been discussed in the Dickinson household.

Despite the obvious dinner table conversations about these issues, and despite the strong beginnings of feminism in England and in New England (and the Dickinson family contacts with women and men who were involved in the movement), Emily was not involved.

Why not? The prevailing theories differ, but they center around the speculation that she was disappointed in love. They differ also over which person wounded her and caused her to stay in her room for decades.

Emily's seclusion has been attributed to her father's powerful influence over her and his forbidding her to marry (although there is no evidence of the latter). It has been attributed to the fact that she was not very pretty and hence could not marry (although the world is filled with physically unattractive women who have found husbands). Her seclusion has been attributed to her being in love with a married and hence unavailable man. This is probably not the case, first of all because there is no hard evidence that such a man actually existed, and second because, even in the Puritan New England of that time, such a romance probably would not have kept a sorrowing poet in her room for a quarter of a century.

Much has been written about Emily's being in love with a woman, a hopeless situation because of the difficulty of lesbian relationships during that time, and because the woman she presumably loved did not return her passion. But we must keep in mind, when we speculate about the possibility of a lesbian relationship, that lesbian is often a code word for feminist. That Dickinson was woman-defined, that she eschewed the traditional womanly pursuits (marriage and children), and that she was very much her own person would certainly give rise to speculation that she was not a "real woman."

In any case, we believe that it probably was not unrequited love that kept Dickinson in seclusion for decades, but her keen awareness of the difficulties, of the lack of place for her, in entering the world.

Women have always been biologically defined. It is said that the moving force behind female actions, or indeed the moving force behind inaction, is interpersonal relations. Men have died and worms have eaten them, but not for love. Not so with women. It is easier to assume that a woman goes into hiding because her relationship with a love object has not worked out than that she does so for causes related to the outside world, often a hostile one.

A friend, intellectual and sophisticated, remarked during a discussion about Dickinson, "Think what she could have accomplished if she hadn't been sick." So, one must speculate.

If Emily Dickinson had not been a recluse, she probably would have married, had several children and several miscarriages, spent her days at the market and at the stove. She might have died in childbirth. In all probability, whether her husband was kindly or tyrannical, whether bearing children left her worn out or in the bloom of health, she would not have written a line of poetry.

Her retirement from the world had a tradition behind it. It has always been an acceptable way of life for spinsters and widows, particularly in New England. Hawthorne's mother was a recluse.

Although hundreds of pages have been written about her father, there is not much written about her mother. We know that she was "endlessly and exclusively domestic, even 'oppressively tidy.' . . . She sometimes embarrassed her daughter by the insistence with which she hovered around guests to inquire if there was not one more cake or cup of tea which would complete their felicity."*

This humiliation over a display of traditional female virtues is decades before its time. Many of the suffragists were more concerned with political and social issues than with an examination of woman's proper role.

* Richard Volney Chase, *Emily Dickinson* (William Sloane Associates, 1951), p. 3.

According to accounts of the Dickinson family, Emily's mother was unusually passive and retiring. Although not housebound in the literal sense, she was a recluse in her own style, the style of thousands of self-effacing Victorian wives. She was not, could not be, the model for Emily. And Emily appeared to crave a model. Her "problem" was that she could not find someone to lead her, to dominate her; as a woman of her time she felt it necessary to have a man to follow, but she simply could not find him. In a letter written in 1862, she laments: "I had no monarch in my life, and cannot rule myself; and when I try to organize, my little force explodes and leaves me bare and charred."*

Throughout her life she found no one to exercise this definitive influence on her. She did have a series of "tutors," as she called them. She called herself the scholar of those men of her acquaintance whom she considered her intellectual superiors. There is some doubt as to whether they actually were her superiors, but this image—learning from wise men—was attractive to her.

The social tradition that says that women can and should learn from men is a strong one. Women should not learn from women, and the greatest taboo is against men learning from women. Women have little trouble securing employment as nursery school teachers, but much trouble indeed securing employment as university professors.

Chase points out that for all her great personal integrity, Dickinson always paid some obeisance to the "little women" cult so popular in the Victorian period. During that time, of course, one of the few careers open to women was perpetual childhood.

It can be seen from her letters that she was ambivalent about her self-imposed isolation. She wrote at age twenty-one, "I put on my bonnet tonight, opened the gate very desperately, and for a little while the suspense was terrible—I think I was held in check by some invisible agent, for I returned to the house without having done any harm!"

* Ibid., p. 67.

Although she was in seclusion, and hence not part of the nineteenth-century revolution of women, she shared with contemporary intellectual women an interest in the position and the status of women. Mrs. Browning and George Eliot, whom she read and admired, were concerned with the status of female intellectuals as well as working women. Emily Dickinson revered Charlotte Brontë, whose work dealt with the threat—spiritual, social, and biological—to women of overbearing men.

In the Dickinson family circle there was a clear hierarchy: Her father was royalty, she was "low." She writes of marriage as a renunciation: The bride puts away her name along with her dolls and her toys.

> *Baptized before without the choice,*
> *But this time, consciously, of Grace*
> *Unto supremest name—*
> *Called to my full—The Crescent dropped—*
> *Existence's whole Arc, filled up,*
> *With one small Diadem.*

Unlike most women of her time, she rejected original sin, and, indeed, most Christian concepts.

> *Of God we ask one favor,*
> *That we may be forgiven—*
> *For what, He is presumed to know—*
> *The Crime, from us, is hidden.*

She believed more in self-determination than most of the men, and certainly the women, of her period. Her biographer writes, "She came uncomfortably close to adumbrating Christian Science."

Her favorite book of the Bible was Revelation, which has traditionally appealed to the poor, the humble, the deprived, and the desolate. The Dickinson family was none of these, and Emily's intellect certainly placed her above the humble. She

was a female, however, and that may have caused her to identify with the oppressed.

In "How many times these low feet staggered" she wrote:

> Stroke the cool forehead, hot so often,
> Lift, if you can, the listless hair;
> Handle the adamantine fingers
> Never a thimble more shall wear.

> Buzz the dull flies on the chamber windows;
> Brave shines the sun through the freckled pane;
> Fearless the cobweb swings from the ceiling—
> Indolent housewife, in daisies lain!

This is a lament about the life of an ordinary woman. "Indo-
lent housewife" can stand for man and all humankind, but in
using the imagery of a thimble, for example, it is likely that
Dickinson was attempting to talk about women's lives.

From 1862 until the end of her life Dickinson was more or
less in seclusion. In 1870 she told her tutor, Higginson, "I do
not cross my father's ground to any house or town." After that
she left the house only to visit her brother and sister-in-law,
who lived next door, occasionally to visit with other close
neighbors, and to work in her garden.

She did not deviate from her idea of herself as a private
person. She treated her poems as letters, refusing to have
them published. During her lifetime only six poems and a
Valentine rhyme were published. She sent them to friends.
Throughout her life she maintained many friendships
through letters and through personal visits. She did not visit,
she was visited.

One of her visitors was Dr. Josiah G. Holland, a writer and
intellectual. Although he was interested in the problems of
women, he was ardently opposed to feminism. He remarked
that the "truly lovable, humble, pure-hearted, God-fearing,
and humanity-loving women" of his acquaintance did not
want the vote. In an essay on "The Beauty and Blessedness of
Female Piety" he wrote: "Young women, this is my last letter
addressed specially to you; and as I take your hand and give

you my adieu, I wish to say a few words." He then stressed the dependence of women because "your bodies are smaller than those of men," and urged them to live in an aura of sunniness, duty, and eternity.

Col. T. W. Higginson was Dickinson's foremost and favorite tutor. She did not regard him very highly as a critic of poetry (her opinion was correct), but she admired his general intellectual prowess. She believed "that everything he uttered in his writings was true." Higginson was educated at Harvard and became a Unitarian minister. Later, declaring that his principles would not allow him to continue in the church, he resigned his pulpit. He was a strong abolitionist.

Perhaps the most significant fact about Higginson, the person Emily Dickinson chose as her mentor above all others, is that he was an ardent feminist. As he had collected songs and stories of the Negro slaves, he collected songs and stories of domestic slaves. In 1867 he wrote in "Literature as an Art": "We seem nearly at the end of those great public wrongs which require a special moral earthquake to end them. Except to secure the ballot for woman—a contest which is thus far advancing very peaceably—there seems nothing left which need absolutely be fought for."

In *Common Sense about Women* he expressed his fear that across the face of America there might pass "the shadow of the harem." He deplored the fact that creative or literary women were the "intellectual Cinderellas" of society and were likely to be ransomed from obscurity late in their careers, if ever. In an essay devoted to "the most eminent poetess of the world," he made Sappho one of his intellectual Cinderellas. The aura of scandal traditionally associated with the name of Sappho, he insisted, must be attributed to the disrepute into which women as a class always fall.

A noteworthy aspect of their relationship is that Higginson tried to interest Dickinson in culture and in women's rights. Both attempts failed. He urged her to attend meetings where papers were read and discussions carried on. He suggested that at the very least she attend a meeting where he was reading his paper on Greek goddesses. She would not go, perhaps out of shyness, perhaps because she realized that she could play no role in achieving equality for women in either the intellectual or the political sphere.

Critics have wondered about Emily's firm friendship with Higginson. Some suggested that his visits and their voluminous correspondence helped to allieviate her loneliness. Certainly she was lonely. However, it is no accident that of all the people on the Eastern seaboard with whom she could have corresponded, she chose him. Because of her family's prominence, and because of her intellect, she could have attracted any number of companions, male or female. Higginson may have been a second- or even third-rate writer, but he was a first-rate champion of women.

Chase does admit that Dickinson had few opportunities open to her other than being a recluse: "If Emily Dickinson wished to observe what sort of life might be open to a woman writer with a background similar to her own who did not become a recluse, Helen Hunt Jackson was an admirable example. Although she obviously had a gift for literature and could sometimes write eloquently, she nevertheless strikes one as an almost classic example of the neurotic writer."*

Mrs. Jackson used several literary names, none of them her own. She was brilliant, impetuous, and a thorough individualist. Her life was plagued by physical illness, personal tragedy, and various compulsions.

Chase compares the two women and concludes, in perhaps one of the most significant statements made about the choices available to women in the nineteenth century, "Contemplating the two women together one senses anew the rightness, for her, of Emily Dickinson's life, the rightness of her jealously guarded privacy and of her strategy of keeping society at arm's length. The feminism of the time, a most striking phenomenon in our history, was surely admirable in many of its ideals. Yet the pitfalls which it offered to creative woman were numerous and dangerous. While it liberated the minds and

---

* Chase, *Emily Dickinson,* p. 286.

lives of some women, it urged others into all sorts of unnatural situations, inventing for them new forms of suffering and breakdown while it imposed upon them the norms of an inferior intellectual culture. These hazards to the talented woman could be clearly seen in the broken and unhappy life of Helen Hunt Jackson. In her decades of skirmishing with Mrs. Jackson and Higginson, we see that Emily Dickinson perceived the dangers offered to her by the feminism as well as by the general culture of the time and that—though she fell far short of perfectly succeeding—she was determined to protect herself and her art."*

There is little doubt that Emily Dickinson perceived the dangers of breaking from traditional sex roles, of becoming a well-known intellectual force, of not marrying, of not bearing children. Her beloved brother and companion, Austin, in his own way suffered from sex-role stereotyping. He was not the severe, aloof, cool man his father was. He is said to have bent over his father's coffin, kissed his forehead, and said, "There, father, I never dared to do that while you were living."

It is not completely clear whether Higginson, with his feminist orientation, tried to get Emily out of the house to enter a more public life, or actually discouraged her. For example, although he read her poetry to public gatherings, Thomas Johnson, who edited her letters, believes that Higginson told her in 1862 that her poetry was not good enough for publication and that she accepted his judgment.

Emily Dickinson was removed from the events of her day. For example, she wrote to a friend on the eve of the first election of President Cleveland: "Before I write to you again, we shall have had a new Czar. Is the Sister a Patriot? 'George Washington was the Father of his Country'—'George Who?' That sums all Politics to me." As an American who could not vote, it was rather witty to call Grover Cleveland her sister.

In her poetry Dickinson emphasizes power. Rebecca Pat-

---

* Ibid., p. 292.

terson, one of her biographers, believes that she knew how
lacking she was in power:

> She knew that her position was weak almost to impo-
> tence—not merely against her parents but, far more impor-
> tantly, against the entire world.
>
> . . . Someone has suggested that many a woman an-
> ciently burned as a witch was in truth a vigorous, gifted
> woman with no outlet for her abilities. Again and again Emily
> wrote uncomfortably that she was too "large" for her environ-
> ment; her own explanation of herself is worth noting. She
> faced a world that was hostile to everything she wanted to do,
> inimical to the realization of herself, and she fought it with the
> only weapon in her possession—withdrawal.*

> *Born—Bridalled—Shrouded—*
> *In a Day—*
> *Tri Victory*
> *"My Husband"—women say—*
> *Stroking the Melody—*
> *Is this—the way?*

Dickinson writes, clearly, of her view of marriage, and its
similarity to death for a woman:

> *Rearrange a "Wife's" affection!*
> *When they dislocate my Brain!*
> *Amputate my freckled Bosom!*
> *Make me bearded like a man!*

Chase says "she gave to her seclusion a range of significance beyond herself and beyond her family circle. Her antag-
onist was nothing less than society itself, and the public opinion through which the values of society were forced upon the

---

* Rebecca Patterson, *The Riddle of Emily Dickinson* (Boston: Houghton
Mifflin, 1951), p. xii.

individual. She was entirely content to be what the world called a 'nobody' so long as her position as 'nobody' could be used as a vantage point of attack. And in her way she defeated the world, finally overwhelming its most stubbornly held redoubts. . . . Emily Dickinson's seclusion—sad as it was and unpropitious for our culture—was yet one of the notable public acts of our history."*

She knew what was outside, and she chose to stay in.

Dickinson's niece Martha tells of visiting Emily in her corner bedroom on the second floor of her home, and of how her aunt made as if to lock the door with an imaginary key. She turned it, and said, "Matty: here's freedom."

Adrienne Rich discusses Dickinson's seclusion. "Even from men, New England took its psychic toll; many of its geniuses seemed peculiar in one way or another, particularly along the lines of social intercourse."**

Hawthorne, until he married, ate his meals in his bedroom, apart from the family. Despite the connections made by the mental health professionals about good living and family meals, many people involved in creative work have found the regularity, inevitability, and frequent dullness of family meals counterproductive to their work. Thoreau demanded solitude and geographic restriction, and recommended such a life-style to other writers.

Dickinson's seclusion is not ignored by Rich. She believes the poet was too strong for her environment. She concludes: "To say 'yes' to her powers was not simply a major act of nonconformity in the nineteenth century; even in our time it has been assumed that Emily Dickinson, not patriarchal society, was 'the problem.' The more we come to recognize the unwritten and written laws and taboos underpinning patri-

---

* Chase, *Emily Dickinson*, pp. 268–69.
** Adrienne Rich, *On Lies, Secrets, and Silence: Selected Prose 1966-78* (New York: W. W. Norton, 1979). p. 160.

archy, the less problematical, surely, will seem the methods she chose."*

The seclusion was not ignored, but neither was it analyzed. Thoreau may have gone off to Walden Pond; Hawthorne may have taken his meals alone. But the symbolic action of one of the great poets of the nineteenth century, who was also a woman, deciding to spend her life in the home, the woman's province in all centuries, cannot be passed over. Rich shows us how hostile the world outside the home was for women, but not how meaningful that particular choice was for Dickinson.

Higginson is casually mentioned in Rich's essay. But again his presence in Dickinson's life is not analyzed. Rich believes that Dickinson's devotion to women has purposefully been disregarded by her biographers, who, even if not puritanical, hesitate to give credibility to female bonding. This is no doubt true.

But the relationship with Higginson cannot be dismissed. He was an outspoken feminist, a promoter of women and women's rights. And Dickinson chose him as her mentor from a wide range of candidates—New England was full of literary types. It is likely that in her desire to show Dickinson as woman-identified, Rich failed to recognize the importance of her also being identified with a male feminist.

A startling fact about Dickinson's life is that despite living in a family much concerned with worldly affairs, she herself did not talk of the world outside. Perhaps a form of agoraphobia, but affecting more women, is a type of existential agoraphobia: not being allowed to talk about the outside world.

There are a whole range of worldly issues, both past and present, that impinge upon the individual apart from the day-to-day mechanics of interpersonal relations. These encompass war and peace, justice, racism, sexism, economic distribution, social status, and a myriad of forces that distinguish human existence from that of a goldfish or a carrot. Like a soldier on a battlefield cut down by fire he neither sees nor hears, or an industrial worker sick and dying because of chemicals worked

* Ibid., p. 183.

with decades ago, these worldly issues do determine our daily lives, perhaps even more than our known and visible companions or surroundings. Refusal to speak about them may be the most serious kind of agoraphobia.

Emma Bovary tried to broaden her small world by taking lovers. As Flaubert explained to us, that was no solution for the bourgeoise European housewife—her life became so tangled and unsatisfying that she ended it by taking poison.

6

Other Women Who Chose to Stay Home:
A Most Unlikely Radical Feminist and an Artist

THE TRAUMA OF EVENTLESSNESS

This young woman agoraphobic is by background, temperament, and seeming passivity an unlikely person to have a purpose or a cause; she is even less likely to need treatment by mystification, drugs, or hospitalization. A timid twenty-eight-year-old housewife was referred for psychotherapy by her family physician after she failed to respond to a variety of tranquilizers and sedatives. Her presenting symptoms were fear of losing her mind, episodes of severe apprehension in the street, feelings of panic in department stores, supermarkets, and beauty parlors, and terror that she might harm her three-year-old daughter.

She related that she was the elder of two children, having a brother five years younger than she. Her parents were Russian Orthodox immigrants from Eastern Europe. Her father had advanced to a semi-managerial position in a small paternalistic company. Her mother worked periodically to supplement the family income. The patient was brought up under strict discipline: She was a docile child and adolescent, properly obedient and respectful of her parents. Her father worried about her outside activities and fretted about some of her girlfriends. He often met her after school to see that she did not stray into corrupting circles of teenagers. Even though her social life was restricted, she managed to have some friends of both sexes. She never evidenced any rebelliousness.

After high school there was no mention of college, although she had done fairly well in her courses. Instead, her father got her a job as a stenographer in the company where he worked. No one asked her if she would like to work, or at what; it was assumed that any girl would be grateful for such a job.

At work she met a young engineering student who worked there during the summer. Her father thought this was a fine match, and he did everything to encourage the relationship. The young man graduated and they were married. He returned to this same company as a full-time employee; after the marriage, she left her job. A daughter was born soon thereafter. The external circumstances of her life appeared ideal—she had a husband who was good to her and who had a bright future, satisfied parents, a nice home, and a healthy baby.

Concurrently her younger brother was approaching manhood. The course of his life, however, contrasted sharply with hers. An inferior student in high school, he was nonetheless encouraged to go to college. He was fully supported financially. With some continuing academic difficulties, he graduated and was immediately hired by an architectural firm at a good starting salary. There was no suggestion that he join the father's company, which was considered beneath his talents.

Three years after the birth of her daughter, the patient responded to her seemingly ideal external conditions with apprehension and panic. This puzzled everyone and enraged her father, who did not want his daughter to be a burden to his son-in-law. The patient found no friendly listener among her relatives—they interpreted her sadness and fearfulness as signs of selfishness and ingratitude. "Doesn't she have everything? What more does she want?" Yet she was beset with attacks of anxiety.

"I'm afraid something is going to happen but I don't know what it is." As her life story unfolded, it became apparent that her timidity and docility had naturally deprived her of adventuresomeness, choice-making, and even minimal self-determination. She had not even become pregnant out of wedlock, as her father feared. Her present and her future were reasonably assured.

What had she to fear? She was well adjusted, accepted by her friends and family, loved by her husband, fulfilled as a woman and mother. There were certainly no external dangers; she had more security than the average person. Internal dangers, of course, might include fear of sexual feelings long repressed or contaminated by earlier parental threats and warnings. Then there was fear of harming her daughter, an obsessive thought that might too readily be interpreted as sadistic. Her anxiety must be a reaction to danger from within; deductively there being none from without.

Closer scrutiny of her life revealed that pressure was being put on her to have another child; her daughter was now close to three and would "like a baby brother." The grandfather spoke again and again that no family is complete without a male child and that he had money put away for a grandson's college education. Nothing was said about any equivalent treatment for the granddaughter. It was in this setting that her symptoms appeared, one of which was the fear of harming her daughter.

At this point, it was becoming apparent to her that unless something changed, her life would be one of dependence and submission, secure and protected, bereft of any excitement, challenge, or adventure. In a word, eventless.

She had suffered being eclipsed by a favored brother; was she to be a witness and accessory to another, similar crime? In her apprehensive exclamation "Something is going to happen, but I don't know what it is," she was secretly lamenting the danger that the opposite would be true, that in her life nothing would happen. She had been caught in a secure trap with the courage neither to complain directly nor to extricate herself. Her life at home, in the streets, and in the stores was devoid of deprivation, predatory human beings, or ferocious animals. Instead the absence of challenge, of decision-making, of problem-solving would be her destiny. Even her three-year-old daughter appeared self-sufficient, engaging only a small part of her time and attention.

A trauma, in psychoanalysis, is generally difficult to define. Broadly speaking, it is thought to be a "startling experience, a shock, with lasting effects." The traditionally held view of trauma has as its chief distinguishing components a stimulus from without or within that overwhelms the ego, leading to various symptoms and incapacitation of the person.

We contend that the very opposite, the absence of stimuli, can be traumatic. A lack of external events and appropriate internal responses can constitute a trauma no less than dramatic assaults against the ego. More than that, the anticipation of more and more eventlessness may similarly constitute a danger of severe proportions to one's well-being. The woman under discussion "broke down" at the point when she painfully realized that without some change or correction her future would be a continuation of a past characterized by submission to authority, absence of choice, and a general exclusion and isolation from the significant stimuli of life. Consistent with psychoanalytic theory, her anxiety contained the anticipatory repetition of the traumas of the past. Was she irrational to fear that her future would be as intellectually and emotionally constricted as her past?

The contrasting fate of her brother proved to be a precipitating factor in this woman's belated rebellion. This was no neurotic sibling rivalry but a realistic, objective appraisal of the inequities attending the raising of a son and daughter in a family of limited socioeconomic circumstances, where the son is held to be a dividend, the daughter a mortgage, as the ancient Greeks might tell us. Credit for intelligence, judgment, choice-making, and self-determination that was lavished on the son never was accorded the daughter. Not one to complain, she nonetheless felt the injustice and responded with her cryptic alarm and protest.

Similarly, her untoward thoughts about her daughter originated not so much from pent-up sexualized or deneutralized aggression as from chagrin over the fate of the female. Was her daughter to be destroyed as she thought herself to be? Would destiny impel her to foist upon her daughter the inequities she herself felt?

These are real dangers, external dangers, but they are not readily apparent. We cannot declare them either unreal or internal simply because they are not universally perceived or acknowledged. Often the therapist is still listening with the third ear when the times call for a fourth.

The course of psychotherapy was in large measure predictable. For a long period she both affirmed and disclaimed her boredom, her dissatisfaction, and her own insignificance. She asked the question put to her by her husband, her parents, and her own superego: Why she? Why was everyone else in her circumstances content with life? No one else had to go to a doctor. When would she be able to stop going?

Was she really indulging herself by receiving a talking treatment? And was she in truth going through an infatuation with the doctor when she should have her mind on her family and household chores?

The area of greatest suspicion was the absence of medication in the therapy. She knew there are now miracle drugs that bring contentment. The doctor seemed to be agitating rather than relieving. The husband began to contemplate what might happen to the marriage. Yet with new insights she began to observe and note that all was not so tranquil with others in her circumstances. It became a source of pride for her to recognize new aspects of living and forces that were acting on her and others. Her husband, predictably, felt that if she would simply change her attitude all would be well. In this, there was inordinate pressure for tranquilizers so that she would no longer be disruptive. When she finally became aware of her legitimate struggle against disappearance, her physical symptoms largely abated and her energies were channeled into areas that might change her plight. This eventually was encouraging to the husband who earlier in the illness had been at the end of his rope and wondered whether she should be hospitalized.

Was her past disturbing? Yes. In her early years her parents were in the throes of elevating themselves from poverty. Both

parents worked hard and were always anxious lest the fragile
progress be impeded. The children had to be well disciplined
and protected from the temptations and exposures that bring
social disaster. The father was a determined worker who
never deviated from the proper behavior and decorum his
boss demanded. At times it was touch and go but gradually he
became a member of the team and felt a modicum of security.
Overhanging his existence, however, was his lack of formal
education; he felt the pressure of the new employees, now
almost all college graduates. Here he was confronted with his
ambivalence toward education.

On the one hand, determined that his own son receive the
best education possible, he was conscious of his own deficiencies and inadequacies vis-à-vis the upcoming young men
"who could write a decent letter when they had to." Yet if he
reluctantly and painfully saw the necessity of education for his
son, his pride could not allow his daughter to have more
education than he. In this time of life, as if learning from Lear,
he would not have a daughter lording it over him. His frustrations were unevenly distributed, landing on the female, as
typifies worldly priorities. For him, a girl was a success if she
caused no trouble or disgrace, as well a girl might. He had
heard that girls off at college are apt to go wild, losing respect
for parents and bringing shame to the family name. It would
not do for the son to have a sister who was a tramp. Elevation
to the middle class had come hard enough, and he was afraid
to tempt the fates.

She became daddy's girl and frequently was the only one
in the family who could talk back to him, but only about incon-
sequential matters. She was solicitous of her brother and
sought to protect him from the wrath of their father on his
infrequent occasions of rebelliousness. Toward her mother
she was similarly solicitous, but felt neither awe nor affection.
Her father was the ultimate figure of authority who would
determine her destiny.

In her teens the sexual threat, the specter of going wrong,
was constant and made sex loathsome, mysterious, and in-
triguing. Her one great power was to undo; her father made

her aware of this. At times his very preoccupation with sex appeared to her as a command. She felt he was almost disappointed that she was not adventuresome in this area.

Similarly, by all conventional standards her relations with other people were adequate. The family, particularly the father, breathed a sigh of relief; the ordeal of carrying a daughter through the pitfalls of adolescence ended in success. Obviously the father's preoccupation was a manifestation of the repressed sexual problems of fathers and daughters, but social pressures as well as class prejudices also helped determine his attitude and behavior. Her obeisance was more apparent than real. Unexpectedly, she became aware that she was paying too high a price for the needs, real or fancied, of others. Her neurosis, developing as it did, was her rebellion. She was not spoiled by success as some would say. Instead she sought to save herself from annihilation by a self-preserving negativism, a refusal to become the possession and vassal of still another man (her husband) who would take her for granted. She could not, with her training and timidity, become a "bad" woman to show her protest. What was left to her was more of the same, to exaggerate her timidity to a fault, literally to become afraid of her own shadow. How much more feminine and passive can one get? She summed up her own dilemma: "I don't want to be forgotten."

Attuned as we are to the threats of untoward nefarious drives from within and catastrophic events from without, we may forget the despair that comes from the prospect of a passionless and unchallenging existence. The trauma of eventlessness, of nothing at all ever happening, can be a catastrophe of major proportions. As Thomas Carlyle observed: "The tragedy of life is not so much what men suffer, but rather what they miss."

There are many kinds of death; the biological is but one. People worry about their survival: professional, social, and political, as well as biological. Loss of self encompasses matters of quality of living, accomplishments or the lack of them, meeting or falling short of one's ego-ideals, and, to be sure, relations with other people. Failures here are as relevant and crucial in fostering hopelessness as the knowledge of one's inevitable demise. We hold with Kierkegaard that we are always well aware of the loss of a limb, a wife, or a five-dollar bill. But, the loss of self in its many subtle manifestations and forms is not well understood. The self slips away and only the fortunate get a warning signal.

This woman was anticipating, or perhaps reporting, her own social and psychological death. Luckily, she was anxious about her destiny and cried out against what might seem its inevitability. Her anxiety was salutary and self-preservative; she would "not go gentle into that good night."

This woman's symptoms allowed her to separate herself from the fate of the young women with whom she grew up and who now surrounded her in the suburbs. She withdrew from the role of shopper and hair-dryer captive. In her home, she held her ground by having but one child, no small feat in light of the persistent pressures of husband (don't you love me?), relatives, friends, and the church. If not for having children, why women?

Limited by lack of education and worldly experience, her positive accomplishments were modest. She was able to work part-time as a door-to-door canvasser for a research corporation. This was surely not world-shaking but nonetheless it puzzled and dismayed her relatives who deemed such work dangerous for a woman, especially since it brought her into inner-city districts. Plagued by anxiety in supermarkets and beauty salons, she suffered no fear in this outside work, only exhilaration, giving evidence once again that the overriding danger to her existence lay in the safety of the housewife's role. The hostile elements of her environment were not the people of the street but her loved ones who saw her as pure biology.

Therapy encouraged the actualization of her worldly aspirations. A woman's destiny might indeed be broadened. She began to feel human and rational. Until then her family and friends had perceived her as insane at best, misanthropic at worst. Incidentally, there was a fortuitous assist from the fast-moving events of the world; with the new urgency for population control, her insistence on not having more children now appeared not entirely nonsensical and selfish to some around her.

Beset with the fear of harming her child, she could not possibly have another since her fitness as a mother was in doubt. How could a helpless infant be entrusted to her care? No, her father would have to forego his craving for a grandson and find contentment in his granddaughter. The money put away would have to go toward her education. And, there were no more children. The family resources eventually went for the one female grandchild.

It was only after everyone accepted her determination not to have any more children that her street fears subsided, and with a vengeance. After many years of needing someone to accompany her on the smallest excursion, she got a job that required her to walk in the streets, very often after dark. Her family was as deeply upset and concerned for her safety as they had been formerly with her inability to leave her home. Her stubbornness reminded them of her father. She remained laconic and inscrutable, never rendering opinions or explanations about her behavior as if to let others figure her out as they wished. Her one great interest continued to be her daughter, who was on the way to a career in medicine.

This woman didn't know who Susan B. Anthony was, had barely heard of Betty Friedan. There was no family tradition of political activity or public militancy of any kind. The mere mention of women's liberation in her circles brought forth condemnation and ridicule. In her family, a woman was fortunate indeed if she found a husband to support her. She had none of the words to express dissent from the prevailing and accepted family expectations of what a woman is and has to be.

Today she watches the vast changes taking place in the world without participating, but stubbornly holds on to the private changes that she and her neurosis have wrought. A radical feminist?

CAROLYN WYETH

Timing is of great importance for those who decide to stay at home, as it is for the moment of emergence. In the case described above, the person could emerge only when it had been established that her daughter, the doctor, would receive the family's resources.

Agoraphobia affects all classes of people, for a variety of reasons. The interpretation depends upon seizing the implication of the act and its timing. Take, for example, Carolyn Wyeth, who decided to emerge at age sixty-nine after decades of painting in solitude.

The Wyeth family's founder was N. C., the great illustrator whose interpretations of such books as *Kidnapped* and *Treasure Island* are now classics. His son, Andrew, was honored with a one-person show at the Metropolitan Museum of Art in New York in 1975. Andrew's son Jamie is a noted portrait painter whose subjects range from John Kennedy to Andy Warhol. N. C.'s daughter Henriette is also an accomplished painter. Another daughter, Ann, is a composer. N. C.'s third daughter, Carolyn, retreated early in life behind a shield of privacy.

Carolyn was the protégé of her father. She shared many of his characteristics, including a revulsion toward sham and an attraction to nature. A farmer who lived near the Wyeths relates: "One time Miss Carolyn and Mr. Wyeth were going to some art show in West Chester and they asked me to ride along. So I did. Then they said come on in to the show, but I didn't want to, you know. I wasn't dressed for it at all. I just had some old clothes on and I said no, I didn't want to go in, but, you know, they just made me go in there, me looking like a farmer just off a tractor in there with those tuxedos and things. It embarrassed me, it did. And those fancy people too, I wouldn't wonder. But Mr. Wyeth and Miss Carolyn, they never worry about such things."*

* Gene Logsdon, *Wyeth People, A Portrait of Andrew Wyeth as He Is Seen by His Friends and Neighbors* (New York: Doubleday, 1971), p. 138.

The Wyeths were a close-knit, talented family who had a sense of their worth. By the time Carolyn was an adult (thirty years old), her father had acknowledged her genius: "Carolyn has just completed the Keats' mask still life, and both Andy [her brother] and I believe it to be an *astounding* canvas. If she never painted another thing, this will record a truly important talent. This may sound florid, but I'm sure of what I'm saying."*

Her talent was also recognized by Horace Pippin, the outstanding primitive artist. He preferred her work to that of any other member of her gifted family. Her father records the event: "I've had an astonishing time with Horace Pippin. I can't possibly tell you about it adequately now; I'll only tell you that after looking at many of mine, some of Andy's, and Henriette's, he looked at Carolyn's 'Keats' with real excitement and wonderment, blew a long low whistle and said, very slowly, and solemnly, 'Now, *that there's* a sensible picture.' "**

Her father once described her as "an enthusiastic anarchist, pugilist—and angel—who pounds through the days like a war horse." Carolyn did not like to go to school; she preferred to stay at home and draw or play with her animals.

Carolyn's family was dignified and discreet; perhaps she learned from them that her appetites and behavior were too strong for most of her world. She withdrew to her personal world, bounded by the property line of her father's home in Chadds Ford, Pennsylvania.

In January 1979 she agreed to a large retrospective show of her paintings at the Brandywine River Museum in Chadds Ford. In conjunction with the show, she was interviewed by Richard Meryman of *The New York Times*:

No, I'm not exactly a recluse . . . but nearly so . . . as close as I can be. . . . I think the best thing is a quiet life. In the morning when I have my coffee with the dogs lying

* *The Wyeths, The Letters of Newell Convers Wyeth, 1901–45* (Boston: Gambit Press, 1971), p. 801.
** Ibid., p. 803.

around, I'll be quiet just thinking about my picture, thinking
about what I'm going to paint, how I'm going to do it. It's a
quiet that Thoreau—I hate his term but he's right—called a
"divine greening."

Somebody busts in here, just starts talking and chattering,
it breaks into that mood, balls me up. Takes me an hour to
simmer down. My father . . . just talking to people at the post
office . . . that would break into his thoughts, and his hand
would start to shake when he went out to the studio.

Growing up in a period when "other-directedness" was
not only the vogue, but the prescription for mental health,
Carolyn must have found it difficult to stick to her art. What
she knew, what her father recognized, is that no one can be
creative at a party. Bureaucracies may give needed jobs to
many people, but a commitee never invented anything.

Those who want to organize or even reorganize knowledge
or beauty must do it alone. And they must fight, particularly as
children, to keep their privacy. She told Meryman: "I think all
great stuff comes out of being alone. At the time you may feel
lonely, but it's doing something wonderful to you. If you have
that till you're 12 or 14, boy, you're all right. You can really
dream; you've got that child in you all your life."

Whereas the greatest obstruction to privacy for the creative
boy is probably being pushed outside to play baseball, the
greatest obstacle for a woman may be marriage. Carolyn "was
married for a few years . . . but that's no good for a woman
artist. I needed that aloneness. Anyway, I'm too damn independent to be married."

Society has dictated not only that married women have as
their main job serving others in the household, but that proof
of their competence as mothers and wives, and as women, is
that they are always, permanently, on call. The physician carries around a beeper; the mother is supposed to have a sixth
sense that tells her her child is in trouble, whether in a distant
room in the house or in a distant city.

Mothers of small children usually do not have the luxury of
getting the flu, let alone working on a project that requires

more than a few minutes' concentration. The generally accepted reason for the popularity of fiction in women's magazines is that the paragraphs are short and each story can be read in twenty sittings. Such is not the case with the average novel.

Biographers have tried to suggest that N. C. had an unnatural and overbearing attitude to Carolyn. An issue of *American Artist* devoted to the Wyeth family describes their relationship: "A studio constructed for Carolyn adjoined N. C. Wyeth's own, and she worked here under the stern tutelage of her father. She could hear him pace back and forth toward his canvas and then away again, his energy inexhaustible, while she slowly worked and worked her own drawing. If his footsteps approached the direction of her studio, she accelerated her movements to impress him when he entered the room. On one occasion he found her reading the newspaper . . . and admonished her severely for wasting time."*

N. C. respected his daughter's work and took it seriously, unlike his attitude toward other women and their work. In his letters, for example, he talks about how his wife did not give him the emotional support he needed:

> I did not specify that it was the peculiar sympathy and belief from a fellow *man* that I craved. . . . The stimulant from our *men* sympathizers is distinctive (although no more valuable), but it *is distinctive* and plays its special and important part in our lives.
>
> We must agree that it is impossible for a woman to enter into our special work and stand before us to lead—to take the *initiative*.
>
> This power is not woman's, as the past ages in Art and Science testify. But they can bless us with a spirit of love and faith that supersedes all other stimulus or encouragement. In the proportion that a man and wife individually do their part well, in that proportion are they a *spiritual* aid to one another.

* *American Artist* 39, 391 (February 1975).

And I believe this to be the only vital spiritual aid that can be transmitted between man and wife.*

N. C. and Carolyn had a special relationship; she was there to do more than encourage him, give him love and faith. She was there to be a great artist. The biographers have suggested that he was too hard on her. But perhaps he was trying to save her from the usual fate of talented women—eventually neither they nor the world take their work seriously.

Her older sister, Henriette, for example, was also a talented artist. N. C. wrote to his mother about her: "Henriette, let me tell you, Mama, is *astounding* in her powers of perception and her sense of logical reasoning, and you should see her *fight* to help wipe the dishes, and brush up the floor."** Henriette was a student at the art school connected with the Museum of Art of Boston; she later studied at the Pennsylvania Academy of the Fine Arts. She suffered from poliomyelitis, which left her right hand permanently damaged.

Carolyn's younger sister, Ann, was also an artist, and a composer as well. In December 1934 her "Christmas Fantasy" was played by the Philadelphia Orchestra, conducted by Leopold Stokowski.

Ann and Henriette both married artists, and each had three children. As the other children in the family moved on, Carolyn remained at home with her parents, beyond her father's death in 1945 and her mother's in 1973. She painted over one hundred works. She has been called by critics "the best painter in the family" and "the strongest woman artist in America today."†

The conventional wisdom would question the mental health of a father who incessantly pushed his daughter's talents. The wisdom that acknowledges women's fate as serious professionals might recognize that he was trying to save her.

---

* *The Wyeths*, p. 390.
** Ibid., p. 410.
† *American Artist*, February 1975.

The conventional wisdom would question the mental health of staying at home all those years to paint. Those who grasp the daily schedule of the wife and mother might wonder whether these hundred paintings would have been created if Carolyn Wyeth had led a conventional life.

When Carolyn placed her work on exhibit in January 1979 the Associated Press reported: "Carolyn Wyeth has lived in the shadows of the men in her family. . . . This week, however, she stepped into the sunlight."

Carolyn stepped into the sunlight as soon as it was safe.

7

A Queen Who Chose to Stay at Home: The Deferential Imperative

There is a long tradition of survivor's guilt. Widows throwing themselves on their husbands' funeral pyres is not a myth. When a husband dies, a woman often feels (and sometimes is told) that she didn't take good enough care of him.

Some religious traditions hold that a widow should not go out in public, should not show her face, for a specified period of time. After the death of Prince Albert, Queen Victoria suffered from agoraphobia for the rest of her life. There is no question that her culture and she herself were ambivalent toward women and power; how this ambivalence showed itself is a fascinating case history.

The popular image of Queen Victoria is of a strong, stern, practical person. She was anything but that. She suffered from the numerous common illnesses of the nineteenth century, watched countless of her loved ones die, and was ambivalent at best about the correctness of a woman's running an empire. She was also romantic to a high degree.

After the death of Prince Albert she stayed in seclusion for decades, a seclusion that profoundly affected political and social affairs of state. Her reasons for seclusion remain her secret; this lack of mobility is barely alluded to in her letters and memoranda. She ran the empire from her rooms; she did little traveling but kept her grasp on events all over the world.

Victoria had had a cloistered childhood: "Morning and evening, day and night, there was no relaxation of the maternal vigilance. The child grew into the girl, the girl into the young woman; but still she slept in her mother's bedroom; still she had no place allowed her where she might sit or work by herself. An extraordinary watchfulness surrounded her every step: up to the day of her accession, she never went downstairs without someone beside her holding her hand."* It was not until she became queen that she moved into her own quarters.

Her biographer, Lytton Strachey, conveys the general attitude to women of the period, and particularly to women of power:

> It was her misfortune that the mental atmosphere which surrounded her during these years of adolescence was almost entirely feminine. No father, no brother, was there to break in upon the gentle monotony of the daily round with impetuosity, with rudeness, with careless laughter and wafts of freedom from the outside world. The Princess was never called by a voice that was loud and growling; never felt, as a matter of course, a hard rough cheek on her own soft one; never climbed a wall with a boy.
>   . . . Henceforward female duty, female elegance, female enthusiasm, hemmed her completely in; and her spirit, amid the enclosing folds, was hardly reached by those two great influences, without which no growing life can truly prosper—humor and imagination.**

After she became queen, she grew to love privacy and power. Although smitten with love and greatly attracted to Albert, she took to her bed immediately before the wedding. She ran a fever and the royal physician thought she was coming down with the measles.

---

* Lytton Strachey, *Queen Victoria* (New York: Harcourt Brace Jovanovich, 1921), pp. 43–46.
** Ibid., p. 151.

It was not the measles that were attacking her, but a very different malady; she was suddenly prostrated by alarm, regret, and doubt. For two years she had been her own mistress—the two happiest years, by far, of her life. And now it was all to end! She was to come under an alien domination— she would have to promise that she would honour and obey . . . someone, who might, after all, thwart her, oppose her— and how dreadful that would be!

. . . No doubt, she loved Albert; but she loved power too.*

Strachey ends the description of Victoria's terror: "He reappeared, in an exquisite uniform, and her hesitations melted in his presence like mist before the sun."

Victoria lived for decades after the death of Albert. Her love of power, even during widowhood, was carefully shrouded in presumed deference to Albert: "I am anxious to repeat *one* thing," she wrote her uncle, "and *that one* is *my firm* resolve, my *irrevocable decision,* that *his* wishes—*his plans*—about everything, *his* views about *every* thing are to be *my law!* And *no human power* will make me swerve from *what he* decided and wished."** Victoria made sure that she would be the absolute ruler after Albert's death—because *he* wanted it that way. A most convenient way to eliminate the meddling of uncles and cousins.

Strachey described how Victoria became a recluse after Albert's death:

Her cheerfulness did not return. For months, for years, she continued in settled gloom. Her life became one of almost complete seclusion. Arrayed in thickest *crepe,* she passed dolefully from Windsor to Osborne, from Osborne to Balmoral. Rarely visiting the capital, refusing to take any part in the ceremonies of state, shutting herself off from the slightest intercourse with society, she became almost as unknown to her subjects as some potentate of the East.

* Ibid.
** Ibid.

> . . . Her place was in the inmost shrine of the house of mourning—where she alone had the right to enter, where she could feel the effluence of a mysterious presence, and interpret, however faintly and feebly, the promptings of a still living soul.*

Victoria's social seclusion had implications not only for high society, but for business and industry as well. She deprived the populace of its pageantry, and the effect on the dressmaking, millinery, and hosiery trades was disastrous!

Early in 1864 word spread that Her Majesty was about to go out of mourning, and there was much rejoicing. It turned out to be a rumor and Victoria wrote to *The Times* to say so:

> This idea cannot be too explicitly contradicted. The Queen heartily appreciates the desire of her subjects to see her, and whatever she *can* do to gratify them in this loyal and affectionate wish, she *will* do.
>
> . . . But there were other and higher duties than those of mere representation which are now thrown upon the Queen, alone and unassisted—duties which she cannot neglect without injury to the public service, which weigh unceasingly upon her, overwhelming her with work and anxiety.**

The popular discontent with Victoria's uninterrupted seclusion burst out in the shape of republicanism. Radical opinion in England, stimulated by the fall of Napoleon III and the establishment of a republican government in France, grew extreme. The monarchy was attacked both in theory and in practice at a vital point: It was declared to be too expensive. Victoria's retirement gave weight to the argument. It was pointed out that the ceremonial functions of the Crown had virtually lapsed. If the queen didn't go out, where and how did she spend £385,000 a year?

It was only after the general election of 1886, when Victoria's forces swept the election, that she abandoned her long

* Ibid., pp. 305–6.
** *The Times*, London, April 6, 1864.

seclusion. She threw herself into a multitude of public activities. She appeared in drawing rooms, at concerts, at reviews. She laid foundation stones, she went to Scotland. Her deference to the dead Albert finally receded.

It was not that he was forgotten—that would have been impossible—but that the void created by his absence grew less agonising, and even, at last, less obvious. At last Victoria found it possible to regret the bad weather without immediately reflecting that her "dear Albert always said we would not alter it, but must leave it as it was"; she could even enjoy a good breakfast without considering how "dear Albert" would have liked the buttered eggs.

And, as that figure slowly faded, its place was taken, inevitably, by Victoria's own. Her being, revolving for so many years round an external object, now changed its motion and found its centre in itself.

. . . Her egotism proclaimed its rights.*

Victoria gave her name to the period of John Stuart Mill and Charles Darwin. Yet she was totally removed from the social movement of her time. Toward the smallest and the greatest changes she remained inflexible. She never withdrew her opposition to smoking. Kings, bishops, and ambassadors, invited to Windsor Castle, were forced to smoke secretly in their bedrooms. Sir Theodore Martin gives us his firsthand account of this powerful sovereign's view of the emancipation of women. The mere mention of such a proposal sent the blood rushing to her head. She wrote to Mr. Martin: "The Queen is most anxious to enlist everyone who can speak or write to join in checking this mad, wicked folly of 'Women's Rights,' with all its attendant horrors, on which her poor feeble sex is bent, forgetting every sense of womanly feeling and propriety. Lady _____ ought to get a good *whipping*. It is a subject which makes the Queen so furious that she cannot contain herself. God created men and women different—then let them remain each in their own position. Tennyson has

* Strachey, *Queen Victoria*, p. 385.

some beautiful lines on the difference of men and women in 'The Princess.' Woman would become the most hateful, heartless, and disgusting of human beings were she allowed to unsex herself; and where would be the protection which man was intended to give the weaker sex?"*

When Victoria finally emerged from mourning—Victoria who did not allow smoking in the palace, who called upon God to assure the differences between the sexes, who quoted Albert at breakfast, lunch, and dinner—she emerged with a friend and constant companion, one John Brown.

Brown, who had entered her service as a stablehand and had risen to become her permanent attendant, was with her at all times. When she resumed social dancing after thirteen years of mourning, he was her regular partner.

After Albert's death, Victoria stayed in Balmoral Castle where she was completely hidden from view, for four months each year. John Brown was her righthand man and, many believed, he ruled the Empire. Victoria expressed dread and loathing when the time came each year to leave Balmoral: "What had happened to cause this heartsickness? Granted that she hated Windsor Castle, which she once likened to a 'living grave,' this would hardly account for the violence of her reaction. Why did she regret leaving Balmoral 'more vividly than I did last year'? When this admission is seen in context one cannot help but wonder if it did not have something to do with the man whom she had just appointed to be her special servant, who had had 'everything to do for me,' as she told her daughter, and whom she would not be seeing for another year."**

In time, Brown's influence extended even to Victoria's travels abroad; the queen arranged her itineraries to avoid those countries where he was not well received. For example, the

---

* *Queen Victoria as I Knew Her* (1908).
** Tom Cullen, *The Empress Brown, The True Story of a Victorian Scandal* (Boston: Houghton Mifflin, 1969), p. 48.

queen usually journeyed to Germany via Cherbourg and Paris, bypassing Brussels, because the Belgian court persisted in treating Brown as a mere lackey. In Germany Victoria insisted wherever she went that a suite of rooms be set aside for him, preferably near her own suite.

Victoria, worried that she sought solace from Brown, asked Dean Wellesley if her accepting comfort from him was wrong. The Dean told her a "settled mournful resignation" was better than acute grief. He reassured her "that God saw fit to put in our way comforters with 'congenial natures' and special healing powers and we should not question His wisdom." It is interesting to note that the ruler of an empire must ask one man's permission to pursue a friendship with another, following the death of the man she considered her mentor, despite the fact that Albert was a German who never even made a pretense of ruling the British Empire.

Brown was blamed for the queen's seclusion. "Brown would not let her come. Brown would not let her out." A Swiss newspaper wrote that they were secretly married, and that she was going to have his child. The British minister in Berne promptly lodged a complaint against the newspaper with the Swiss government.

Victoria used several lines of attack to maintain her seclusion and her power. "In this persistence of the Queen, we may detect the real reason why the Cabinet was determined to make an end of the agitation by yielding to it. The Ministers were unwilling to oppose her, because they were afraid, with good cause, of endangering her health. In July 1867 Dr. Jenner made to Lord Derby an alarming statement of the Queen's condition.

"Here is the passage taken from Lord John's journal, dated 6th July 1867: 'Lord Derby opened with a very alarming statement of the Queen's mental and bodily condition. Dr. Jenner had told him that any excitement produces the most severe bilious derangement, which induces vomiting to an incredible extent, and his fear is that if relief fails the mischief would fly to the head. . . . Jenner has offered to come before the Cabinet to be examined.'"* Her second line of defense was that there was no room at any of the royal residences to entertain notables properly. She wrote that she would be quite willing to do her part "if the country would build her a Palace for the purpose of lodging foreign Royalties, and make her a handsome allowance for entertaining them."

Cullen writes that her preferred female social companion was the wife of her head keeper, who talked about her children and tea cakes. She avoided the wife of an historian with whom she had social acquaintance because it required preparation: "She might suddenly ask me whether I approved of female doctors."

As Victoria was romantic about her relationships with men, she was unrelenting in her disapproval of independent women. She said of one woman in the court, who hunted in Africa, that she was a "female Nimrod and unladylike." She wrote against what was called "rational dress reform," the right of women to wear trousers.

When Brown died, Victoria again went into intense mourning. When she had been criticized for not emerging after Albert's death, she developed "flying gout." After Brown's death, her knee made it impossible for her to walk. After the swelling went down, she still could not walk; the doctors concluded that her troubles were at least partly psychogenic.

She was sensitive about her semi-invalid state and banished all male members of the household from the dinner table. She did not want the outside world, nor the men in the palace, to see her being carried about.

It is not important whether John Brown was Victoria's lover or merely her constant companion. What is important to note is that this woman who headed a powerful empire seemed unable to do so without the aid, or perceived aid, of a male. She considered herself a member of the weaker sex, although she certainly was in no way frail. She ran the empire, deflecting the advances of her male cousins and uncles, on the

---

* Charles Whibley, *Lord John Manners and His Friends* (London: W. Blackwood, 1925), vol. 2, p. 121.

ground that Albert (who had been dead for decades) wanted the empire run in a certain way, and she would see to it. Yet she always maintained that ruling the empire was not a job for a woman.

She wrote to Gladstone on February 14, 1874: "People are apt to forget that the Queen is a *woman,* who has far more on her hands, and far more to try mind and body, than is good *for any one* of her sex."*

We do not know to what extent Victoria depended on Albert, and later on John Brown, to help her make decisions, to help her be queen. It is safe to assume, however, that the public probably minimized her own contributions and maximized her dependence on men and on men's minds. Throughout history women who acted and thought independently have been said to be following the directions of men.

As a woman's place has always been seen as the home, those women who left their homes to act and think in the broader world did so with the justification that this activity was merely an extension of their roles in the home.

* George Earle Buckle, ed., *The Letters of Queen Victoria* (New York: Longmans, Green, 1926).

8

Anorexia Nervosa: Never Too Thin

Unjust—unjust! said my reason, forced by the agonizing
stimulus into precocious though transitory power; and
Resolve, equally wrought up, instigated some strange
expedient to achieve escape from insupportable
oppression—as running away, or if that could not be
effected, never eating or drinking more, and letting
myself die.

Jane Eyre at Age 10

A woman can never be too rich or too thin, so the saying
goes. Actually, the thin part of the equation is recent.

Throughout most of human history there was not enough to
eat. Looking substantial was a sign of prosperity and hence a
status symbol. From 1500 until 1900 body weight and volume
had a strong visual appeal for both men and women. Upper-
class qualities included slim hands, feet, and noses, but heavy
bodies.

The Rubens ideal was voluptuous, and no doubt thin
women of that period felt self-conscious. Today all that has
changed. A recent television movie about fat and its horrors
depicted a woman whose husband left her, for the most part
because she had grown fat and unattractive. "When we make
love," he told her, "I pretend you look like you did ten years
ago." This woman weighed 139 pounds. Today's most popular
topics of conversation, and the most popular books, are about
diet, exercise, jogging, and the beauty of bones. These subjects affect both men and women, but there is no doubt the
impact is stronger on women.

The television commercial suggesting the "pinch test" to
determine whether one must eat a particular low-calorie
breakfast cereal shows a very slim woman discovering that she

can pinch some flesh on her sides, indicating that she is too fat. It also shows her distinctly chubby husband pinching his sides, where a more substantial handful can be held. Both husband and wife laugh at his fat; hers is no laughing matter.

Medical and beauty authorities differ on what constitutes a healthy body or a beautiful one. But one condition—anorexia nervosa—is attracting increased attention. There is no dis-agreement that a person starving to death is neither beautiful nor healthy.

More and more young women are developing this condi-tion. They stop eating, lose weight, and eventually lose their appetites. Some are hospitalized and force-fed. The condition has been "diagnosed" in a variety of ways, usually centering around the parent-child conflict over autonomy, or perhaps over unresolved Oedipal strivings. Mother (the dispenser of food and therefore a convenient villain) is often given coun-seling along with her starving daughter.

A glimpse into how anorexia takes hold of a young girl is found in *Solitaire* by Aimee Liu. The author describes her "progression" from a 130-pound attractive, popular, honor stu-dent to an 89-pound person, obsessed with dieting, thinking she is fat, and measuring every ounce she consumed. She vomited, fasted, used laxatives. She was sure, even at 89 pounds, that she was too fat. This all went on during her high school years and through her first year at Yale. Finally, she saw the error of her ways and began to eat. Fortunately, her parents had not had her hospitalized and force-fed as had the parents of many of her friends in similar circumstances.

Aimee Liu's father worked for the United Nations. From age three to five she lived in India, where she must have been aware (as are even the children who don't live there) that most of the children are starving. Another factor in her preoccupa-tion: Her grandmother once called her "chubby." However, the major reason for her diet, only barely touched upon in her book, is that the preoccupation of all the girls in her wealthy suburban high school was their weight. All thought they were too fat. There is little they can affect or control in their lives, except their weight.

The constant downward trend [of the scale] somehow comforts me, gives visible proof that I can exert control if I elect to. It is the greatest satisfaction in my life. . . .

This was not our first discussion on the topic of my weight. My parents have been pleading with me to eat more since they first realized that I was under one hundred pounds. But to no avail, for I am adamant. My diet is the one sector of my life over which I and I alone wield total control. I *enjoy* counting calories and feeling skinny. No one can force me to become fat again!*

During the course of this trial she became a fashion model, seemingly an unusual profession for a high school honor student who doesn't need the money—until we consider the culture of the female high school student: glamor is all and grades count for little.

In her top-flight high school, the greatest competition between the girls was not grades, not even boys; it was dieting. Each classmate who stops eating represents a threat: She may become the thinnest person in the class. The thin competition was understood to some degree by Aimee, who speculated that one of her friends would not give up eating: "She was a dancer and an outdoor girl, and she enjoyed eating too much ever to give it up. And maybe most important of all, she was involved in too many other projects and dreams to dwell on calorie counting and exercise. She was what you'd call a well-balanced human being."**

There were not many well-balanced human females in the school. Aimee overheard her mother bemoaning her starvation on the telephone: "The reinforcement certainly hasn't helped matters any. You go over to the high school today, and it's like walking into a concentration camp."

Aimee fell in love with Ken, a young man who would be attending the same college. Her view of male-female relationships "sucked me in, filled me with romantic yearning that

---

* Aimee Liu, *Solitaire* (New York: Harper & Row, 1979), pp. 46–7.
** Ibid., p. 121.

bordered on mawkishness, but it felt wonderful. I would become his slave, and he would become my mentor."

But even her slave status (having a "steady" has always been highly regarded) was not enough to make Aimee relax. She and another "concentration camp survivor" were discussing why they were threatening to those who were not on diets: "They're in awe of us. It sounds insane, but maybe it's something like celebrity. Everybody wants to be thin, after all. Right? Including the doctors, and our mothers, and our friends. We've achieved what they can't."*

At Yale, Aimee realized there were other important contributions she could make to the world and pleasures she could enjoy besides dieting and having a steady relationship with Ken. She recognized that she was so unsure of herself that she had even tried to get him to marry her at age eighteen: "That moment of dread . . . was the slow horror that I had begged for entrapment and that my passion for self-denial was on the verge of destroying both our lives. Marriage negated every dream I'd ever cherished for a future life, and yet I'd proposed so glibly, almost unconsciously!"**

If Aimee Liu was the only attractive and scholarly young woman who starved herself almost to death, if she was the only one who tried to get married at age eighteen (saved only by her boyfriend's refusal), we could assume she had a personal emotional problem. But all over the country girls are eagerly celebrating "becoming his slave" with engagement rings and church weddings.

It is no accident that those who suffer from anorexia nervosa are mostly girls. They see on television and the movies that skinny is good and not-skinny is disaster. Strength and power, which would be more likely to accompany a person weighing 130 than 89, are not touted as virtues for women.

The usual explanation for anorexia is that the parents, particularly the mother, provide a less than ideal environment at

* Ibid., p. 188.
** Ibid., p. 213.

the family dinner table, and thus the girl stops eating in protest, so she can show that she has some power over her own life. The problem is indeed power, but not power in the nuclear family constellation. It is power, or rather their lack of it, in the world. The 89-pound girls in the suburbs, people who apparently have everything going for them—money, brains, looks—are giving a message when they stop eating. They are telling us that if we measure their worth by their reedlike shapes, they will show us just how painfully reedlike a shape can be.

As agoraphobia has been misdiagnosed and mistreated— and not recognized as the metaphor it is—so too with anorexia nervosa. There has been some faint recognition that the patients refuse to recognize their condition as an illness.

Hilde Bruch, one of the world's experts on anorexia, reports "they have never felt better; they complain of nothing, do not realize they are ill and have no wish to be cured."* There has been no acknowledgment on the part of the experts that there is nothing to "cure."

Mara Selvini Palazzoli gives a basically sound analysis. She states the obvious: The current Western psychosis about slimness provides the basis for the obsession to take root: "The pressure on women, especially middle-class women, has never been greater: that they are expected to have unisex energy, to perform as brilliantly in a career as in running a home, to be good lovers as well as good students—all earlier and earlier. For the type of girl who becomes anorexic, unlimited choice can mean unlimited pressure to achieve. If the Victorian girl became hysteric because of the stifling of her energies, the contemporary anorexics may retreat into illness because of the demands made on them. And she is found more often in middle-class than in working-class families; that is where social and parental demands are strongest, where food has lost its primary value as something worked hard for and

* Hilde Bruch, *The Golden Cage: The Enigma of Anorexia Nervosa* (Cambridge: Harvard University Press, 1978).

good to eat, and becomes a part of the behavior game."* This explanation misses the point that being very thin is not the style for the poor, who still equate being thin with not having enough to eat.

In an essay on anorexia, Rosemary Dinnage rightly criticizes the present treatment of the condition, which centers on family therapy and behavioristic games: "The families are certainly more bewildered and docile in letting themselves be filmed, taped, slapped on the back, called by their Christian names, shifted around the room, told what sort of people they are, and sent off to do 'homework' for a set time each day to change the family habits."**

Hilde Bruch notes, "When they begin to diet, they seem to be doing nothing different from what thousands of other women are doing. How does it happen that they go too far?" The answer is probably that they go too far because they are performing a caricature: If the world says women should be thin, they will be *really* thin.

There are two glaring omissions in all the analyses of anorexia. First, it is never explained why practically all anorexics are female; second, although the family and home settings are explored in minute detail, the world outside the family, where the girl will participate in adult life, is virtually ignored. Bruch comments:

> We can only speculate why it affects the well-to-do and has become so much more prevalent during the last fifteen or twenty years. . . . I am inclined to relate it to the enormous emphasis that Fashion places on slimness.
>   . . . Another related factor seems to be the justified claim to women to have fuller freedom to use their talents and abilities. Growing girls can experience this liberation as a demand and feel that they *have* to do something outstanding. Many of my patients have expressed the feeling that they are over-

* Mara Selvini Palazzoli, *Self-Starvation: From Individual to Family Therapy in the Treatment of Anorexia Nervosa* (New York: Jason Aronson).

** Rosemary Dinnage, "The Starved Self," *The New York Review of Books*, February 22, 1979.

whelmed by the vast number of potential opportunities available to them which they "ought" to fulfill, that there were too many choices and they had been afraid of not choosing correctly.*

The image of only rich girls becoming anorexic is probably due to the fact that private practitioners and hospitals connected to universities see people from that socioeconomic group. It is unlikely the girls go on a hunger strike because they have too many opportunities; more likely, they see too few. They are usually bright and good students. It would be particularly agonizing for them to realize that their fates are circumscribed.

These people are not crazy: The emphasis on thinness for teenage girls, and women generally, is ever-present in every social class. Parents of teenagers—especially mothers, since they are the ones who do the major socializing job on their daughters—reprimand them when they gain weight. After all, men don't want fat wives.

Anorexia is not only a hunger strike, it is a strike against the nurturant role of women. These girls are telling the world in no uncertain terms that they will not be like their mothers, they will not cook for people, they will not attend to the biological needs of a family. No eating, no cooking.

Bruch centers much of her attention on the families of the anorexic girls:

> A conspicuous feature of these families was the paucity of sons. More than two-thirds of these families had daughters only. Most denied that this posed any problems, though one mother became so depressed for having given birth to a fourth daughter, having disappointed her husband by not giving him a son, that the father had to take care of the little girl; he raised her with the precision of his professional training as an electrical engineer. In another case the patient was convinced that not having a son had not been a problem for her father, that he took pride in his daughters, that he treated them intellectually

---

* *Golden Cage*, p. viii.

as sons; he was particularly proud that they all knew how to throw a ball "correctly" (namely, like a boy).

. . . It is significant that the fathers value their daughters for their intellectual brilliance and athletic achievements; rarely if ever do they pay attention to their appearance as they grow into womanhood, though they will criticize them for becoming plump.*

Many of the anorexic girls' mothers had been career women who felt they had sacrificed their aspirations for the good of the family. In spite of superior intelligence and education, practically all had given up their careers when they married. They were also often unusually weight conscious (not unreasonable among women who had given up their private aspirations for the "feminine" role in life).

The "golden cage" may not be golden at all, but simply a cage. One of Bruch's patients was impatient with her own mother "because she saw in her what she dreaded would be her own fate—to be a nothing, to be devoted to a husband, to be devoted to her children, but without a life of her own." Another felt that "being born a girl had put her at a disadvantage with her parents, particularly her father." The doctor comments:

These girls cannot experience themselves as unified or self-directed individuals, entitled to lead a life of their own. . . . Though few express it openly, they had felt throughout their lives that being a female was an unjust disadvantage, and they dreamed of doing well in areas considered more respected and worthwhile because they were "masculine."**

These are not the skewed perceptions of disturbed teenage girls. Few women are entitled to lead lives of their own; watching their own mothers would teach them that. The more worthwhile areas in our society are thought to be those in which men participate. Anorexics say that they feel "humili-

* Ibid., p. 24.
** Ibid., p. 55.

ated by the procedure of being coerced into stuffing . . .
against their will." And well they should.

Bruch points out that "on principle, anorexic patients resist
treatment." Of course they do. They are giving a message;
they don't consider themselves sick.

One of the gravest errors in treating anorexia is the limited
scope of the examination. Even with psychiatrists who don't
prescribe drugs, behavior therapy, or force-feeding, there is a
tendency to look to the meaning of the act, but to look no
further than the hapless family. Was the mother overprotec-
tive? Did the father spend enough time with his children?
Was a brother given more attention? These issues, although
pertinent to a person's life, are not as pertinent as the fate the
young girl expects for herself. She correctly perceives that all
her scholastic and intellectual accomplishments count for
nothing.

Gandhi, Dick Gregory, Cesar Chavez—these men have
gone on hunger strikes, and whereas not everyone agrees with
their politics or views justice and equality with their eyes, no
one doubts their sanity or the sincerity of their protests. The
girl who goes on her hunger strike is also fasting as an act of
revolt. She is telling with her body what she doesn't have the
language, or perhaps the courage, to tell with words. She is
saying I don't have to be lean and beautiful and get good
grades and have a good social life, so that I can marry a fine
boy and stay lean and beautiful and raise children and entertain my husband's colleagues and worry about whether my
daughter will also be lean and beautiful and get good grades
so she can marry a fine boy and have babies. I am putting the
brakes on all this for a while.

Not everyone will, or should, agree with her politics or her
form of expression. Not everyone will agree with her mode of
communicating revolt. But no one should doubt what she is
doing and what she is saying. No one should force-feed or
hospitalize her. And no one should suggest she is mentally ill.

According to Douglas H. Ingram, Physician-in-Charge,
Obesity Program, The Karen Horney Clinic, fat women seeking psychiatric assistance for weight reduction outnumber fat

men by about ten to one. For women, keeping slim is not only connected with aesthetics and with health, it is part of survival, economic survival.

And girls have to be carefully taught—early. An analysis of the camp advertisements in *The New York Times Magazine* (winter and spring 1979, 1980, 1981, 1982) shows a distinct difference in what constitutes physical fitness for girls and for boys. Boys are offered: All Sports Camp where every boy plays and every boy learns; baseball, basketball, soccer, football, hockey, track, riflery, tennis, golf, swimming; National Football Players Association camp; Instructional Football Camp (offense, defense); Body Building Camp; Ted Williams Baseball Camp. For the girls: For a summer's fun that can change your life: Lose Weight, Lose 20–45 pounds; Slim 'n Trim Down on a multi-million-dollar college campus; Overweight (slight or quite)—the original weight control camp for girls; Overweight girls, lose weight the fun way, starting age 6 years, slenderize, charm; Overweight—girls 8–18 will love being losers at Camp Stanley, the original slim-down luxury summer camp; Overweight girls, complete camp program in the Catskills, average loss 15–30 inches.

Hilde Bruch typically writes: "For long-range recovery [of anorexia nervosa] the whole pattern of family interaction needs to change."*

It may be sad and difficult when the patient can't go out of the house, but it is really tragic when the psychotherapist cannot leave the house—in vision and for subsequent interpretations. For long-range recovery, changing the pattern of *family* interaction will not be enough. There must also be change in the world.

* *Psychiatric Spectator,* 11, 9 (1979): 4–5.

9

Gendermandering: Our Experts' Contribution to Agoraphobia

According to the latest statistics, only 7 percent of Americans live in what was previously considered the American family—a working father, a full-time homemaking mother, and dependent children. What was previously thought of as natural, inborn, biological, or instinctual has been proved to be fiction. The proof is coming not from our laboratories or seminars but in vivo from our homes, streets, offices, factories, and athletic fields. What only a few years ago we knew was masculine or feminine behavior, now must be reappraised. Ironically, the last to understand the changes are the "gender experts." Not content to define what is male or female, they still insist on defining what is feminine and masculine and, more than that, they still stress the biology of these metaphors. As new evidence comes in, their intransigence hardens; in the parlance of politics, they stonewall it.

No one can argue with the legitimate search for knowledge and dissemination of information. But in the area of sex and gender research in the United States, conclusions are drawn from the flimsiest evidence. Furthermore, these conclusions form the basis for interventions and therapies (intrusive social engineering) that with few exceptions become the rationale for the continuation of sexist attitudes. This is particularly dangerous because these rationales come from "experts" in prestigious medical schools and universities.

The literature of the gender experts exhibits a semantic error that they of all people should not make: They equate male with masculine and female with feminine. They know that being male or female has largely to do with anatomy, whereas masculine and feminine should refer to complexities of gender, combining the social and psychological as well as anatomical. They speak of "masculinizing" hormones when they should be saying hormones that produce male organs or male physical qualities. Why this obfuscation? The victim of these experts is the "feminine" boy (never mind about the "masculine" girl). Despite mild disclaimers, we cannot help but see their disdain of things thought to be feminine. Androgyny, which they refer to as the unisex movement, is considered a deviation. Finally, they conclude from their research that masculine and feminine attributes, not just maleness or femaleness, are determined in utero; that these characteristics are determined by biology, with the implication that making changes after birth would be tantamount to tampering with the natural processes. The bottom line is that if the male is dominant, intelligent, aggressive, and career-seeking, and the female submissive, passive, dependent, and homebound, all these are what *nature* intended.

As further proof, they remind us that it has been this way from time immemorial everywhere on our planet; therefore, these attributes, advantages, and shortcomings must be biologically determined. In this scheme, the dependent male or the career-seeking female is either deviant or, more charitably, a variant. Another issue that arises is their inexorable crusade against male homosexuality, which easily matches and even outpaces the homophobia met with in the most remote backwash in America. "Rough and tumble" is to be the fate of normal boys; any evidence of passivity, sensitivity, or gentleness must be extirpated (this is the integral part of the therapy for feminine boys). The therapy is, by any standards, chauvinism. The protocols, page after page, are informed by a war on anything feminine in a male. The "feminine" boy might become homosexual, which would foredoom him to a hopeless, intolerable, diseased existence.

Conclusions of gender experts have far-reaching effects on mental health attitudes and become incorporated into therapy modalities. For years therapists have used gender polarities as givens as well as salutary therapeutic goals. All too often they have viewed cross-strivings of the male and female as part of a "sick" pattern. We now know from experience, and from illuminating studies about the double standard of mental health that exists in the helping professions, the often crippling effects this has had on women, men, homosexuals, and heterosexuals. The gender experts have become part of our problem.

Milton Diamond hypothesizes that sex differences in the brain are established within four to five weeks after conception under the influence of genetic and hormonal factors and that this will mediate the individual's reproductive and sexual patterns. The latter include his and her behavior that reveals maleness (aggression, assertiveness) or femaleness (subtlety, passivity, dependence). Diamond does not stop here; he tells us that the effects of hormonally induced brain organization include "erotic response levels, arousability, genital mechanisms, sexual identity, and sex-related biases in the spontaneous initiation or acceptance of various activities as well as choice of sexual objects."*

He describes the sex-related patterns: Boys without encouragement choose those activities that require masculinity and stamina, e.g., running, climbing, and wrestling. Girls select relatively less strenuous and conservative activities, e.g., hopping, jumping, playing house, and mothering dolls. We are told that boys are intrinsically more competitive and at the same time better able to cooperate among themselves. Boys are more gregarious; they play in larger groups. We know this

---

* Milton Diamond, "Human Sexual Development: Biological Foundations for Social Development," in *Human Sexuality in Four Perspectives,* ed. Frank A. Beach (Baltimore: Johns Hopkins University Press, 1977), pp. 22–61.

to be so because no culture has girls' games or activities such as baseball, rugby, football, or soccer. Again Diamond insists that these general behavior patterns are innate; any exceptions must be considered deviations.

Are we really supposed to believe that four to five weeks after conception the female fetus shows that subtlety and wisdom of character to step aside and allow the male later in life to monopolize all the high-paying jobs of the world? Does this very same innate subtlety and passivity then work to exclude her from the Constitution of the United States, thereupon depending on the male for direction and domination (for dependency, we are told, is also one of her innate qualities)? And since we can never count on her to be able either to compete or cooperate in groups as large as ten or twelve, we react out of sheer wisdom in excluding her from places like Congress, the Supreme Court, and even the PTA. The game of bridge is just about right because of the numerical imperative as well as the inside activity and low stamina that it requires.

And what of the boy who is not competitive, aggressive, or gregarious? Is he a miscreant? Little wonder that boys have literally had to kill and maim themselves in some athletics and other high-risk physical activities to fulfill these biological imperatives.

John Money, perhaps the most respected expert in the gender field, gives more leeway for free will and personal choice. But he too places great stock in the primacy of hormones and prenatal conditioning. He too takes semantic liberties with regard to anatomy and behavior patterns. Money refers to progestin-induced hermaphrodism. To prevent miscarriages, some pregnant women were given this hormone. This in turn caused hermaphrodism (ambiguous genital organs) in the newborns. These babies are usually reared as girls. Money calls these infants genetic females "masculinized" in utero. He goes on to state that these girls have a high chance of being tomboys. We are to presume that the prenatal hormone determined what he apparently considers aberrant behavior. It is instructive to read his list of tomboyish characteristics:

1. Tomboyish girls like to join with boys in outdoor sports. Groups of girls do not offer equivalent alternatives, nor do their toys.
2. Self-assertiveness in competition for dominance is strong enough to permit successful rivalry with boys.
3. Self-adornment is spurned in favor of functionalism and utility in clothing, hairstyle, jewelry, and cosmetics. Tomboyish girls generally prefer slacks and shirts to frills and furbelows. Their preferred cosmetic is perfume.
4. Rehearsal of maternalism in the form of doll play is negligible. Later in childhood there is no great enthusiasm for babysitting or any caretaker activities with small children. The prospect for motherhood is not ruled out but to be postponed rather than hastened. The preference is for one or two children, not a large family.
5. Romance and marriage are given second place to achievement and career. There is some unconfirmed evidence to suggest that an abnormally elevated prenatal androgen level enhances IQ. Money reassures us that there is no evidence of lack of erotic response and there is no special likelihood of lesbianism, although bisexuality is a possibility.*

Money might ask why these progestin-induced hermaphroditic girls are more likely to become tomboys than, say, the general population. We do not have to invoke the prenatal demiurge to explain this occurrence, if indeed it is fact. There is a possible psychological reason. The phallus is not merely an anatomical difference; it is an insignia or badge of privilege that always gives its possessor special advantage and opportunity. The "hermaphroditic" child soon learns about this, and perhaps she, possessing more of this valuable organ than females around her, takes courage and frees herself from the culturally imposed limitations and restrictions on female children. Money doesn't consider this sociophysiological variable as a possibility, but rushes for the biological explanation with the zeal of a theologian expounding the dogma of Original Sin.

---

* "Human Hermaphroditism," in ibid., p. 69.

Dr. Robert J. Stoller presented a paper in 1976 at a meeting of the American Psychoanalytic Association. The audience was instructed in the detection and "exorcism of femininity" in young boys in an all-out effort to prevent male homosexuality. (Nothing was said about female homosexuality.) Some of the criteria were: the desire to wear girls' clothes, use adornments such as jewelry, "has good taste, looks like a girl in them, puts them on spontaneously the first time rather than having them put on him by someone else, and is never sexually excited by them." Other foreboding signs are: plays with dolls, with girls, or *plays creatively*. The prognosis is even worse if he spontaneously requests to play with girls in girls' games, or is accepted by girls. We are alerted to feminine mannerisms: "if he walks, gestures, carries himself, talks and otherwise behaves" like a girl. Here Stoller concedes that the matter of feminine mannerisms is "too complex to describe but easy to observe." In all, it is part of what he calls "malignant" femininity. There is more, but we are warned that it is only a hunch: "A little boy who enjoys the texture of cloth (not just women's apparel) is at risk for gender aberration (if his father is not a tailor)." Dr. Stoller is very explicit indeed, paralleling in this and in many other ways another historical diagnostic tool, the *Malleus Maleficarum*, the handbook of instructions on how to detect and deal with witches in medieval times.

Dr. Stoller's preventive treatment for this condition is as draconian as are his diagnostic criteria. There is to be no equivocation. The young boy is not to be analyzed in the traditional sense; there is no time for that. Instead he is to be given a crash course in masculinity. The boy is to be rescued from the arms of his "malignant" mother who, Stoller finds, hates men with such a passion that she cannot allow her young offspring to develop into one. While the young boy is receiving this intensive care and instruction, the mother, now alone, is to be treated for the depression that inevitably ensues from the separation. Stoller would like the fathers to be treated also, but reports that thus far none has agreed to treatment.

As the young feminine boy is encouraged to be masculine through intensive therapy, there are several signs of progress: He starts fighting with female siblings and peers rather than playing with and imitating them; physical attacks (such as throwing objects) on mother, nightmares, and phobias appear for the first time. Stoller reassures us that "where these might be reasons for treatment in more ordinary children suffering the effects of Oedipal conflict, we look on such manifestations as evidence treatment is already very successful."* Dr. Stoller elaborates his theory in another article: "Sexual excitement is powered by hostility, by the desire to harm someone." Such worthy qualities as good character, beauty, gracefulness, though laudable, may dampen sexual excitement. "Humans are not a very loving species and that is especially so when they make love. Too bad."**

Stoller's theory explains his treatment goals. Only when the feminine boy learns to hate women will he find the sexual excitement to perform the sexual act with them. Despite Stoller's seeming therapeutic accommodation to social reality, with all the misogyny already present in the world there seems little need to instruct any male, feminine or otherwise, to hate women.

Dr. Richard Green, a student of Robert Stoller, has learned well. He is equally adamant about the need to convert feminine boys but is less sanguine in his treatment approach. He does not whisk the child away from his mother but works with the young boy in psychotherapy and uses the parents as surrogate therapists, instructing them in the details of the child's masculinization. The human rights of individuals (children and parents) find no place here; intimidation, coercion, threatening the child to abandon his errant ways take precedence over personal wishes, desires, or liberties. All must be sacrificed to save the feminine boy from the possibilities of homo-

* Robert J. Stoller, "Boyhood Gender Aberrations: Treatment Issues," *Journal of the American Psychoanalytic Association* 26 (1978): 54–58.

** "Sexual Excitement Powered by Hostility," *Los Angeles Times*, December 28, 1978.

sexuality. Anything considered passive, sensitive, gentle, or kind must be eradicated at all costs. The child is given no choice with whom he plays or how. All avenues must lead to being and playing with boys and the play must be typically masculine.

In our present discussion we are not focusing on or judging results of this therapy since the numbers treated are too small and the observations given are too subjective to draw any reliable conclusions. This is especially true in the area of preventive goals where the ultimate long-term outcome is most difficult to determine; besides, secondary or hidden difficulties (displacement, substitution, etc.) can arise from any type of psychological intervention or tampering. We are interested here in the propriety and ethics of the interventions, namely, how far therapists go and properly can go in pursuit of stated goals. Simply put, do the ends justify the means? And even if the goals are generally held to be salutary, beneficial, and wise to the individual, the family, and society, are the means, the messages that we want imprinted on the mind of a client— child or adult—acceptable?

Green has provided us with a protocol of a "feminine" boy whom he treated. The therapy consisted of one-to-one counseling, group therapy, and use of parents as "surrogate-therapists." The following are excerpts from this treatment. The doctor instructs the mother to reward specifically masculine behavior:

MOTHER: In Cub Scouts they were playing a game. It was real boyish and real good. It was fine. In a game he is rough and tough, and he is one of the last ones in there. It's a game where you eliminate people by trying to pull them over a circle, and boy, they yank them and crank them around a whip and make them fall.

DOCTOR: When you see him doing these things, do you tell him that you're pleased and reward him for it? That's the kind of non-athletic boyish behavior I think he should be encouraged in so that he doesn't have to retreat and back off into feminine things.

But this behavior, seemingly a training to produce a member of Hell's Angels, is not enough for the doctor.

DOCTOR: Rather than his being in Cub Scouts, I would still rather see him go into Indian Guides, because that's a father and son instead of mother and son. You've got to get these mothers out of the way. Feminine kids don't need their mothers around.

MOTHER: Just with daddys and boys.

FATHER: Well, I might look at their schedule. I hate to get involved.

There is something distinctly unappealing and disconcerting about the suggestion that the road to heterosexuality for anyone is a tutelage in violence.

MOTHER: How's he seem?

DOCTOR: I think he's doing great. I think he's really much different. One of the things I had him do today is draw a picture. Do you remember who he drew the first time he ever did that? He drew Mary Poppins about three years ago. And today he drew Frankenstein.

In his enthusiasm the doctor did not ponder the possible message that the boy may have been imparting in the Frankenstein drawing. It is, of course, from the Mary Shelley story. Dr. Frankenstein creates a monster who escapes the control of his creator and terrorizes the local populace.

Finally, at the closing session the boy and the doctor reflect on the experience they have gone through.

DOCTOR: Do you remember any other ways you acted as a girl?

BOY: I'd play house, and I'd have a little dolly. I threw it away.

DOCTOR: Did you? When was this?

BOY: I think it was a couple of weeks ago. A little dolly. It was really ugly. I just got so mad I threw it away, 'cause I ripped all the hair off it. I threw the whole thing away.

For the "feminine" boy to perceive the doll as ugly, tear off its hair, and throw it away is progress. The boy may now take his place safely and securely with the multitude, properly identifying with his own sex, now with the proper attitude and feeling toward the female sex.

The effect of these gender experts goes beyond their own clinical interventions. They publish books and papers that influence the training of multitudes in the helping professions. They establish sex and gender institutes and clinics and receive large sums from private foundations and the government. Because they claim expertise, they are sought out by the media and the citizenry for pronouncements on mental health. Little do most people realize just how flimsy and ambiguous is the evidence of both cause and result on which such positive pronouncements are made. And, gravest of all, how uncritically have so many of these opinions been accepted and even integrated into theory and practice in the helping professions. We have been presented not with science, fact, or truth but with personal opinion, all too often the visceral prejudices, sexism, misogyny, and homophobia of the experts. We must now treat them as part of the problem.

The kind of work done by Stoller and Green is questionable, both in content and in form. As to content, many of us have already acknowledged that gender distinctions are not relevant, and certainly there is no cause for panic and despair if people don't fit into the proper box.

The form, however, is one that any responsible therapist should abhor. Using parents as therapists is reckless and manipulative. One parent activity is to list the activities of the boy, classifying them as masculine or feminine. They are trained to grade their sons, giving out rewards, punishments, and fines. If a boy usually takes a role other than father when children are playing house, he now gets points for playing the father. If he assumes a female role, points are taken away.

Green writes, "For example, a positive total of thirty points may be needed for a trip to Disneyland, ten points for staying up an extra hour for an entire week watching TV, and five points for an ice cream treat for dessert." A negative total of five points may result in loss of dessert and ten minus points the loss of a weekend's movie privilege. Privileges withdrawn must not be masculine related, for example, a camping trip with father or swimming lessons. Scores may be kept on a prominently displayed, attractive graph, much in the manner of public billboards that chart progress in a community fund-raising drive.*

No thought is given to why a young boy might not *want* to imitate his father. Perhaps the father is not as nice a person as the mother. Perhaps (and more likely) the boy sees his mother more and therefore naturally identifies with her.

Another strategy allows the child to play with a neighbor girl, his favorite playmate, only after first engaging in an alternative masculine behavior, such as playing with a neighbor boy. The time required playing with the boy in exchange for playing with the girl is progressively increased. One wonders why playing with boys will assure heterosexuality, while playing with girls may lead the poor youth down the path to homosexuality.

Green refers to John Money's use of a similar technique with adult male homosexuals, who are required to spend progressively more time in heterosexual dating before being permitted a homosexual experience. This method of behavior modification is different from working with young boys only in that the homosexual males request it. While we may question an adult's seeking such rules for his own social life, it is his decision. The children are helpless in determining what is happening to them.

The kind of parents who bring their sons to Dr. Green is illustrated by the reward system used for modifying parental behavior: "Parents may put money into a 'kitty' to be with-

* Richard Green, *Sexual Identity Conflict in Children and Adults* (New York: Basic Books, 1974), pp. 274–75.

drawn as a function of their interaction with the feminine boy. The father may draw out money for time spent in an activity with his son; the more time, the more money; and the mother may draw money for time that would have been previously spent with her son but that she has reassigned by promoting his activity with another boy."* Since the parents agree to being treated as naughty children, it is little wonder they submit their children to dangerous games.

The conflicts about gender may well be the core problem in agoraphobia. In the metaphor and caricature inherent in this syndrome, for the disheartened woman everything one inch outside the front door of her home may be conceptualized as masculine and hence unacceptable as something to enter into and with which to identify. Conversely, everything within the walls, as our world and its appointed gender experts have proclaimed, is feminine. The agoraphobic is, if nothing else, legalistic and a strict constructionist.

* Ibid., p. 275.

10

The Healers

The structure of therapy, that is, the medium and ambience in which the therapeutic interaction takes place, is crucial. The way therapist and client behave toward each other may set the stage for promoting a salutary learning experience, or do the opposite. Similarly, the way client and therapist behave toward each other can serve as a paradigm for other relationships in life.

By "behave toward each other" we mean the strict observance of the rights of each other as two responsible adults, not as one healthy and one sick, or one adult and one child, or one master and one slave. This entails a sense of responsibility to observe the rules of any social contract mutually agreed on as well as the nature of the activities to be engaged in. Consonant with our generally accepted tenets of civilized behavior where sensitive and even potentially damaging issues may be dealt with, strict privacy and confidentiality on the part of the therapist is a sine qua non. Without a guarantee or ambience of such protection, sensitive and important issues may not be discussed. In practice, this means one-to-one private sessions and precludes group therapy or the use of tape recorders. Spouses, relatives, or employers should neither be consulted nor interviewed. This is not secrecy but *privacy*, a rare and receding commodity in our human experience but one that is as central to any psychotherapeutic dialogue as the sterile environment is to a surgical procedure. If a client appears cavalier or indifferent about his or her privacy, or gives all sorts of permission for its abrogation, the conscientious therapist must become deeply concerned about why a person would so readily relinquish such a birthright.

Along with privacy, the agoraphobic must be able to communicate with a therapist without the presence or intrusion of third parties. Since the phobia is so often triggered by marriage, the therapist must have no contact whatsoever with the spouse, even if a strong appeal for such a meeting is made by the patient. The patient often wants to prove that she is a child or pawn in the hands of the grownups who are busily and secretly deciding her fate. Sadly, in most of the reported therapies for agoraphobia, this sort of meddling, along with other infantilizations of the patient, is the rule rather than the exception. Fully grown people (women) are told that the outside world is really quite safe and that they have it within themselves to go forward. They are banded together, holding hands, for a shopping trip to Macy's or Gimbel's as a woman's ultimate success.

Consonant with the imperative for good manners in interpersonal relationships, the therapist must never intrude into the life of the patient either by giving direct advice in its conduct or in any way taking an active hand in its management. In the same vein, the therapist must abjure any authority or power that the patient may want to impart; this obviously means that the patient should never be drugged or incarcerated or otherwise placed in the hands of the therapist or any of his surrogates.

Then there is the whole area of folly and humiliation to which we have briefly alluded. This is a delicate and sensitive issue because in this strategem, possibly more than in any other, the patient seeks to show that the therapist (the world) will behave pompously and overbearingly given the slightest opportunity. The agoraphobic's "helplessness" provides this opportunity and one after the other therapists fall into the trap. It becomes a matter of the utmost necessity if any modicum of dignity and integrity is to be preserved that the therapy be therapist-centered: The principal concerns should be the behavior and manners of the therapist, not primarily those of the client. If the therapist treats the patient as a helpless child, if he intrudes in her life, if he in any way informs her of a better way of behaving (based usually on his chauvinism), if he leads her by the hand at home or on the road or across bridges in the typical paternalistic, patronizing, condescending way that he may want to do, he is confirming her worst fears. Similarly, if the therapist is active, and by use of ruses, gimmicks, drugs, torture, or humiliation tries to "break her strike," he will have confirmed the intractable and hopeless condition that male dominance engenders. In all, the agoraphobic finds ironic satisfaction in having her worst fears confirmed by therapists who love to play God. Now she knows that she is not imagining the whole thing; the raw chauvinism of the therapist who takes over, who desensitizes or resensitizes her, is painfully there in bold relief: for by their therapy, ye shall know them.

The agoraphobe often states that she will not venture from the security of the home because of her fear of losing control. It is difficult for her to be more specific. Pressed, she may say she fears going berserk, going out of her mind, or running amok. Generally tied to what is considered a mental or nervous breakdown, she fears public humiliation or disgrace. These manifest expressions betray inner anxieties that may have origins or analogues from infancy to contemporary social and cultural issues. Loss of control may conjure up fears of infantile sphincter laxity, that one might wet or soil oneself, or vomit. Best to remain at home where such accidents will not occur, or if they do, at least they will happen in private.

At a somewhat higher level, loss of control may mean showing outbursts of anger, rage, or tears as an inappropriate reaction to a social situation. One person feared that she would burst into a fit of uncontrollable laughter at the funeral of a close friend or relative; this was her principal communicable reason for avoiding the ceremony. Another feared that she might spew forth a stream of invectives and profanities in church. As we noted earlier there are also fears of losing physical control and of injuring or killing a child.

A ubiquitous fear in the loss of control category has to do with machines: the specter of being unable to steer the car properly, of veering into oncoming traffic, or of lapses in judgment where one would step on the accelerator instead of the brakes, with tragic results. These specters are usually reserved for nightmares. Now they enter daytime "programs," and all are of course possible. However, these are merely the superficial, expressible, communicable anxieties that represent elusive, deeper, and far more meaningful issues. Women fear of loss of control more frequently than men. Losing control has a different meaning for the female than for the male, as a result of societal conditioning. Generally while growing up the girl is made to feel that her prime task is self-control, being quiet, passive, obedient, and silent. Loss of control for her then may mean not being able or no longer wanting to follow this programming. Boys, on the other hand, are taught less about self-control than about the need to control others, the environment, the world.

Enuresis, or bedwetting, is prevalent among boys: More boys have it and have it longer than girls. Similarly, general hyperactivity is greater in boys than girls. These differences in which girls have seemingly greater control have been ascribed to girls' earlier nervous system maturation. It may actually be due to the cultural practice of affording boys more freedom of action and movement.

Girls are expected to have clean and neat rooms, and at an earlier age than their brothers. This carries over to later life: Women are expected to have neater and cleaner homes than men. Men do not apologize for the condition of their quarters or kitchen sinks; women often do so. Schoolteachers don't allow girls the same latitude for running and jumping as they do boys. Standards of posture vary greatly for males and females. Boys are permitted to slouch while girls must sit like little ladies.

If a boy does not show an adventuresome spirit he may

withdraw with loss of hope and self-esteem. So women may feel they will disgrace themselves by revealing inner ambitions, men by showing a lack of them. The anxieties are gender linked and culturally determined. Women are out of control when they are sobbing, shrieking, or trembling. Men out of control are those who have lost their jobs or businesses or markets. A man is said no longer to control the men under him for their talents or products. The lame duck president is said no longer to control his party or Congress. He is out of control as he is out of worldly power. His fate is to retire and be replaced by another who takes charge. It cannot be denied that our gender stereotyping, while it certainly takes its toll among men, is more oppressive to women. It follows then that an "illness" such as agoraphobia, dealing as it does with temptations and its vicissitudes, befalls womankind disproportionately.

Outside the home a woman has no business to mind even when commanded to do so. When she is on the outside and fears loss of control, she may really be saying that women in fact control very little outside of the home. Her fear of losing control away from home may indeed be a pipe dream; she has never had anything out there to lose.

It bears repeating that in our attempts to hide the gross inequities of society, we tend not to face how inimical and inhospitable the outside is for women. It is no coincidence that the sign and reward of cure of agoraphobia is that the woman can again go shopping (one "therapeutic" clinic's graduation present is a trip to Macy's). And it is also no coincidence that the first complaint of the agoraphobe is the fear of going into large department stores or supermarkets, practically the only places where she is accepted.

Women have become so used to being controlled that they often feel it is part of their natures, part of being feminine. They are excluded from dining rooms and clubs, they are harassed on the streets, at colleges they had to submit to rules that never applied to males. Similarly, they were excluded from "male" professions and could not, publicly at least, use the same language as men. Their dress and walk were monitored so that they would not provoke or incite, supposedly a threat to the well-being of the community. These strictures have relaxed, but they have not been eliminated. It is ironic that in a society where it is deemed fit and proper to control women, overtly and subtly, the principal symptom of this disease of women, agoraphobia, should be fear of loss of control.

Several types of maladies befall human beings. The most familiar and simple ones, physical illnesses or injuries, such as pneumonia, a fracture, appendicitis, or diabetes, generally fall within the domain of the medical profession. And although people in such instances may enlist the added support of the deity, medical doctors are given the credit or blame for the outcome. A good result enhances the prestige and power of the medical profession.

Other conditions of physical disease are not so clearcut. The diseases run unpredictable courses; there are natural remissions as well as exacerbations. Many degenerative neurological conditions may run this perplexing course. Multiple sclerosis comes to mind. Some evidence of this disease may appear in the form of paralysis and then disappear for a length of time or never reappear; yet the disease process, however mild, is indubitably present. Or the course may be rapidly downhill leading to severe debilitation and death. Cancer can run a similar course, depending on what tissues are affected and the degree of malignancy. And of course diagnosis itself is far from an exact science. Conditions such as these, and they are numerous, are often ambiguous enough to open the door for all sorts of nonmedical opportunists who are eager to enhance their own power and profits. They rush in when medicine shows signs of faltering or cannot provide the definitive answer or the quick cure.

This is not to defend the medical hegemony that in too many areas has become arrogant, sloppy, and complacent through unjustified credit. Competition here may serve to sharpen skills. However, in the hands of the licensed physician, at the very worst the patient will be protected by some science and some ethical responsibility. This is generally not the case with other "healers."

In many conditions the causation, course, and outcome are not clearcut and lend themselves to other interventions and solutions. There is a vast gray area where the etiology is obscure and uncertain, such as the so-called mental illnesses and psychosomatic disorders. These illnesses are not caused by an invasion of bacteria, a degenerative process, or a physical accident but have to do with many subjective elements connected with psychology, sociology, and history. Here aspects of secondary gain for the individual may play a role; that is, physical illness may play an active role in the solution of a social problem. For example, a young man wanting to avoid the draft might develop hysterical paralysis of an arm. Being bedridden with a chronic back ailment is another way people frequently get out of distasteful situations. It is not incorrect to declare that these instances are nothing more or less than fakery over which the patient has more control than he or she will ever reveal.

Certainly the agoraphobic is faking since she has no organic paralysis of her limbs and will indeed walk out of the house when the spirit moves her or she determines that conditions are right for such a change. We are ultimately correct when we observe that "she could go out if she really wanted to." The situation is more complex than that, but the inhibition to movement is in no way physical or biochemical, our new breed of chemical clinicians notwithstanding. We cannot ignore the matter of the person's will here even though we fully recognize that her behavior is a response to subtle psychological forces and social pressures to which she has no alternative.

Agoraphobics do experience spontaneous recoveries. They may come as a result of subtle changes in one's life that make the illness no longer necessary, or because the energies needed to continue the protest have been expended and the individual must once again conform to the conventional and expected ways of living.

A spontaneous cure poses a grave difficulty for the person: It makes us suspect that the whole illness was fraudulent to begin with. We are no more tolerant of those who pretend to be patients than we are of those who pose as doctors. Both are considered contemptible imposters.

The recovery from the functional illness must therefore involve an outside healer to cover up what might otherwise be considered a willful deception. Even spontaneous recoveries and cures are attributed to healers of varying kinds who are usually eager to play the healing role.

The following account appeared in the *Syracuse Post-Standard*.* It should be noted that the interviewee had received no "psychiatric" treatment prior to her involvement with Recovery.

> It started pretty much right after I got married four years ago.
>
> I started noticing it happening after the first seven or eight months. I just attributed it to the change. I don't adapt well to change. Marriage and a house was a big change.
>
> Suddenly, I found myself unable to go places I used to go to. I couldn't grocery shop. I didn't want to go to the store. And if I did, I was just very, very scared about leaving the house. I didn't want my husband to leave me home alone.
>
> I became fearful of many things I had done so easily before. I couldn't understand why it would happen. I kept thinking it would go away. I thought it was just an adjustment period. But it did not go away.
>
> I didn't seek professional help. I felt guilty to say to my husband, "Look, we've been married just eight months, but I have to go to a psychiatrist. And all the money we've saved to fix up the house we're going to have to spend on me." I felt ashamed. I felt embarrassed. I wanted to work it out myself.
>
> Because I was ashamed, I did not confide in my husband. I did, however, confide in my mother. She just said to me, "Don't worry about it. I'm sure it will go away."

* Reported by John Wisniewski, November 16, 1978. Reprinted by permission.

I could go to work but as far as shopping or anything like that was concerned, I'd get so sick before I'd have to go that my heart would pound. I'd get watery knees. I just sensed danger all around me. I felt that I was going to be mugged or beaten, that something terrible was going to happen to me if I left the house.

The newspaper was a true comfort. I'd pore over it and read articles about women getting mugged downtown. This would reinforce me. "Yes," I'd think, "I have reason to be afraid." I became obsessed with reading about crime.

Sometime later, I read an Ann Landers column. A woman said she was afraid to go places and didn't know why. She said she went to Recovery and is now free of fear and can go anywhere and do anything. I cut the column out and saved it until it practically got yellow. I thought, "That's me," but I didn't want to go to a place where there are mentally ill people. I didn't classify myself in that category. I couldn't.

When my family became so disgusted with me that I felt really alone, I went to Recovery. I had alienated everyone. I lost everybody I cared about. They didn't view me as sick, they just said I was a grumpy, negative person they didn't want to be around.

Sure, I had preconceptions about what Recovery would be like. I had it pictured that there would be people drooling, right out of the hospital, insane, acting violent. I was petrified to go there.

I've been with Recovery for two years now. I don't need Recovery now as much as I once did. But I always make sure I go at least twice a month, because I still have symptoms. When I go places, I sometimes still get the shakiness, I'm looking over my shoulder, feeling a little insecure, a little paranoid.

Because of Recovery, I can drive alone at night now. I still get symptoms at the movies. I don't like strangers close to me. I can endure the movie and sit there without getting sweaty, shaky and in an ugly mood by the time those two hours pass. I'm not saying I'm free of fear and love every aspect of life. I still have a long way to go. But Recovery has brought me to where I am now.

When I was dating, I went everywhere and never had a fear in the world. I lived alone in an apartment and thought nothing of it. Being house-bound didn't come on slowly. It was just there. It hits you like a slap in the face. It's not like a breakdown maybe, where you get warning signals.

Recovery helped me to realize I'm not a kook, not a freak, not going nuts. Recovery helped me to realize I had an over-active imagination that did nothing but detrimental things to me. Recovery helped me to turn my imagination around with more secure thoughts.

This is a typical account. There is the striking contrast between her freedom to move, her freedom from fear during her late adolescence and premarital years and, with marriage, the dramatic, abrupt change. Also characteristic is the almost complete lack of insight or self-reflection on why this should be— "I just attributed it to change. I don't adapt well to change." Marriage and a house were indeed big changes, but she fails to mention the issue of freedom, of the expectations of the marital "contract," nor does she allude to any disappointment. It came out of the blue, after only eight months, an unexpected sickness that, if there were medical bills, might possibly interfere with fixing up the house. There is the inevitable annoyance of husband and relatives who must now bear the burden of her fearfulness and resultant helplessness. It never occurs to her that she is taking out anger and resentment on those who she felt forced her into her present predicament. There is the imperative of giving credit, in this case to Recovery. Without Recovery, we are told, nothing could have been accomplished.

The most pernicious aspect of these "inspirational" groups is that they skirt the truth. Social issues are carefully avoided; examination of such institutions as marriage, divorce, and equal rights are shunned. Everything is geared to a preadult level of thinking and living. Sadly, we can see how attractive this milieu might temporarily be: It effectively separates one's personal plight from worldly or even interpersonal forces. It follows then that the individual will be freed from taking action about circumstances or environment; her troubles have, in effect, no origins. Is it not unfair to say that in a circumstance where ignorance becomes bliss, a process of dehumanization is set in motion that is as bad or worse than the original disease or disorder. As Socrates said, "The unexamined life is not worth living."

The most famous and creative agoraphobe-turned-healer was Mary Baker Eddy, founder of Christian Science.

Her first husband, George Glover, in the building construction business in Charleston, South Carolina, was often forced to trade in slavery. She did all she could to "lessen this evil practice" and wrote articles in Southern newspapers that brought down the wrath of the white community on her. Finally, after his early death, she freed her husband's slaves.

Years later, after the Civil War, she wrote: "Men and women of all climes are still in bondage to material sense, ignorant how to obtain their freedom. The rights of man were vindicated in a single section and the lowest plane of human life when African slavery was abolished in our land. That was only prophetic of further steps toward the banishment of world-wide slavery, found on higher planes of existence, and under more subtle and depraving forms."*

One senses an exquisite and prophetic understanding of liberation that was sorely needed, but as yet had no rhetoric to make it communicable. Eddy was painfully aware of the inequities that plagued the world, of how many battles for liberation were yet to be fought against injustice and oppression, not the least of which was the oppression of women.

Although never as direct in expression for feminism as were such contemporaries as Susan B. Anthony, Elizabeth Cady Stanton, and Lucretia Mott, Mary Baker Eddy worked for women with greater subtlety and tangency as did another contemporary, Elizabeth Blackwell. Both were born and were to die in the same year. Elizabeth Blackwell was the first woman physician in America; she found all doors tightly shut against her. Finally admitted to Geneva College, she gradu-

* Fernand E. d'Humy, "Mary Baker Eddy in a New Light," in *Science and Health* (New York: Library Publishers, 1952), p. 48.

ated at the head of her class.* However, unlike the more militant and nonbelieving Susan B. Anthony, Blackwell felt that God directed her life into medicine, as well as opening medical careers for women.

Thus the two pioneer women healers of nineteenth-century America, whether out of true belief, timidity, or calculated design, remained reverent and deferential. Perhaps in their wisdom they knew that their best chance of achieving their goals for women was in establishing a firm God-linkage to undo or neutralize the succubus image that still prevailed even after the thousand-year Inquisition. Despite her deference and reverence, the hostility toward Elizabeth Blackwell as an educated and fully qualified physician was so great that "she could not find a respectable boarding house willing to let a female doctor's shingle be shown on the premises."** It would not do for a woman in the nineteenth century to say that she wanted to be a physician for the power, the glory, or the personal desire to heal; it had then to be God's direction.

Mary Baker Eddy was born of deeply religious New England parents in 1821 and raised in her grandmother's care. In early childhood she was considered to have a "nervous" temperament. There were voices that would call "Mary, Mary" and no one was there. This was distressing to a strict, authoritarian father who commanded: "Take the books away from her, her brain is too big for her body."†

After she was withdrawn from the ungraded district schools, where the noise and rude pranks of the other children became unbearable for her, she became absorbed with her books at home. Thereafter she was educated by her "spiritually minded" mother and grandmother. Later, her brother Albert, having matriculated at Dartmouth College, educated her; she read with him moral science, natural philosophy, and mastered the Latin, Greek, and Hebrew grammars. Here is one of those rare instances, perhaps paralleling Shelley,

---

* Ibid., p. 12.
** Ibid.

† S. Wilbur, *The Life of Mary Baker Eddy* (Boston: Christian Science Publishing Society, 1938), p. 17.

where a brother did not forget about a sister, an example of genuine filial love.

Mary Baker Eddy was housebound during most of her childhood. Modern clinicians would have diagnosed her as having a "school phobia." Yet her "phobia" resulted in an education that she could never have received at the district schools. Who knows what method lay in madness?

Albert died young and Mary was left to fulfill the obligations of womanhood, principally marriage. The climactic period in her life came during her tumultuous second marriage, to Dr. Daniel Patterson, a dentist who practiced homeopathy along with his dental services. During this marriage she was stricken with a debilitating spinal ailment that rendered her bedridden, with seizures and severe pain that did not respond either to her husband's homeopathy or to allopathic medicine. Her search for health was the impetus for her study and research into medical subjects. However, whatever relief she experienced seemed to come as a response to prayer. Most of these years were spent in invalidism and poverty. Dr. Patterson eventually deserted her, and because of her religious beliefs she was alienated from her family.

It was in or through the person of Phineas Quimby that Mary Baker Eddy was able to change her life and launch a career and a religion that would change the lives of millions of people as well as America itself. At the literal nadir of her life, she "seized the day"—and won.

Phineas Quimby was a mesmerist, a hypnotist, a believer in animal magnetism. He had his supporters and sycophants, but the newspapers called him a charlatan and a quack. Against the wishes of those members of her family who still gave her meager support, she stubbornly insisted on consulting this controversial person who was neither a physician nor a man of God. She lifted herself from her bed and, feeble and exhausted as she was, she presented herself to him at his office in Portland, Maine. Purportedly expecting to meet a man who would heal her through God and religious understanding, she instead explained her invalidism and submitted to his usual hypnotic practice. Her afflictions and pain thereupon disappeared, even to the surprise and amazement of Quimby who apparently became frightened by his own powers. She immediately embarked on a program of educating him on his "mistaken" views. He did, she maintained, in fact effect a cure, not through mesmerism or any other "material illusion but through Christian healing, divine Science."* As the reader can readily anticipate, "divine Science" became "Christian Science." She began "curing" others as she had been cured herself, through the powers of the Spirit.

Mary Baker Eddy was ready for her recovery but had to devise a strategy to turn it to good use. She was shrewd enough to know that no personal benefit would be derived by attributing it either to homeopathy, thus honoring a wayward husband, or to traditional medicine, which even in those times had become overbearing with its barrage of new discoveries and cures. With the emergence of the natural, physical, and medical sciences, religious belief, especially among the intelligentsia, was severely shaken. European philosophers as well as home-grown skeptics were wondering if God really has His hand in any worldly concerns.

What an opportune moment to turn one's recovery into the career and fame that had eluded her so many years. Even in childhood, she had predicted, "When I grow up I shall write a book, and I must be wise to do it." And, of course, from her youngest days, she heard the call from the ether. Later in life she knew that "I shall have a church of my own someday."**

Immediately following her "miraculous" recovery, perhaps sensing what she had wrought, she proceeded to Portland's City Hall and climbed 182 steps to its dome, a symbolic prominence from which she was not to recede.

Mary Baker Eddy was indeed conscious of what can be done with a recovery, that it must be put to good use. "Attributing her well-being entirely to Quimby and asserting he was not a spiritualist or a mesmerist, she wrote two articles for the press of Portland, giving him the honor for her cure and re-

* d'Humy, "Mary Baker Eddy," p. 68.
** Ibid., pp. 22, 1001.

vealing a gratitude so heartfelt and sincere that the most cynical must have admitted her generosity."* (How well she knew that deferring to and honoring a male is very important in getting ahead.)

Little is known of what became of Phineas Quimby. Mary Baker Eddy guessed correctly that although people hungered for cures, they would be offended by the idea of "animal" magnetism. The cure had to be lofty and transcendent yet it should not embarrass with magic and mysticism. She knew she had to strike a medium, however hapless, and go on from there.

A spontaneous, purely self-generated recovery was clearly out of the question. It would smack of immodesty, arrogance, and self-love, attributes poorly tolerated in a woman. Then as now a woman was expected to defer to both man and God. And, without some outside intervention, there is always the suspicion that she might have been malingering from the beginning. And lastly, as those in the field know, "quiet" recoveries make bad miracles.

How beautifully she orchestrated the relationship with Phineas Quimby for her purposes. Giving with one hand to the nonmedical male, she quickly snatched it away with the other. With the necessary modesty and deference she dutifully gave most of the credit to God, leaving some—but just enough—for herself.

Then came the arduous process of building her own reputation and the church that was her goal. There were many obstacles, but her fierce ambition and newfound energies, along with the power and appeal of her message, won for her a host of students. She wisely shared her good fortune with her followers by not only giving them a palatable religion, but for many, careers as practitioners as well. Women now prevailed in the hierarchy.

The importance of the latter cannot be overemphasized as a factor in the church's growth; it was in step with a democratic society. She presented an alternative to the older "plan-

---

* Wilbur, *Life of Mary Baker Eddy*, p. 102.

tation" religions where there was always a sharp distinction between the clergy and laity. How fitting that in the era of Susan B. Anthony and Elizabeth Cady Stanton, a new religion founded by a woman emerged. Eddy insisted that God was neither male nor female. There was now a crack in the patriarchal religious tradition.

Although Christian Science has not caught the fancy of the masses, its membership numbers hundreds of thousands. It has spawned one of the most prestigious newspapers in the country, and was undoubtedly progenitor to much of what was later to be called psychosomatic medicine. For many of its followers, however, the name has more appeal than its practices since disaster has befallen some of those who took the message too literally. Eddy struggled with the medical hegemony, yet desperately desired public credibility. It is interesting to ponder what her reaction would be to contemporary recognition: Blue Cross–Blue Shield, that bastion of medical economic power, now reimburses the clients of Christian Science practitioners.

Today we witness a host of people who have carved careers out of their agoraphobia by being counselors or aides in the quick-cure clinics across the country. Claiming cure or recovery from agoraphobia by a "simple, effective treatment," they proselytize others to follow them. However naive their approach and perceptions, the redeeming part of their largely questionable practices is that there is now meaning and direction to their own lives where formerly there was none. It is probable that this change for the better was the chief ingredient of their purported recovery. The prospect of becoming a professional, helping others, made the difference. At some point in their own therapy they observed that one of the unspoken rewards for overcoming one's fears might be that one would then be chosen as part of a recovery team. Imagine how great this hope would be in a woman who felt she had been trapped in an unproductive, eventless life. The prospect of such an elevation could motivate her nonparalyzed limbs to walk anywhere. All of this, of course, must go unrecognized and unspoken.

11

The Strikebreakers I: Biochemists

Panic attacks may also occur in conjunction with a
depressive illness. At times the panic attacks may be
the original symptom, with the depression supervening.
Most often this involves demoralization in responses to
the travel restrictions and attendant loss of self-esteem
and lacks many of the features of a full-blown
depressive syndrome. On the other hand, the illness
may start with a depression and be complicated by the
subsequent development of panic attacks. According
to the DSM-III guidelines, if panic attacks occur
solely in the context of a depressive episode, then only
a diagnosis of Depressive Disorder is made. However,
if the panic attacks predate the depression, as was the
case with the patient discussed above, then a diagnosis
of Panic Disorder or Agoraphobia with Panic Attacks is
warranted in addition to that of a Depressive Disorder.
However, while demoralized about her functional
impairment, this patient lacked sufficient symptoms to
meet DSM-III criteria for a Major Depressive Disorder.
She was therefore given the secondary DSM-III
diagnosis of "Adjustment Disorder with Depressed
Mood."
M. R. Liebowitz and D. F. Klein,
"Assessment and Treatment of Phobic Anxiety"

MULTIFACETED APPROACH RELIEVES
PHOBIC ANXIETY

Benzodiazepines may be used to relieve the
free-floating anxiety: a monamine oxidase inhibitor or
tricyclic antidepressant may be used to block the actual
panic attacks, and behavior therapy may be used to
assist the patient in overcoming the phobic avoidance,
said Dr. Kessler.

Significant improvement usually occurs after 4

weeks of therapy with an MAO inhibitor, but many
patients continue to improve if treatment is continued
to 12 weeks. Improvement rates have doubled between
the fourth and the eighth week of treatment in some
studies, said Dr. Kessler

*Kenneth A. Kessler, "Multifaceted Therapy
Effective in Phobic Anxiety"*

These excerpts give an accurate picture of the current diagnosis and treatment of agoraphobia by the medical and psychiatric establishment. The therapy is entirely "symptomatic"
(what might be considered practical) and it provides relief for
the patient's ills, if not for the patient. Recently psychiatrists
have begun to find "underlying depression" as the culprit for
so many ills heretofore disguised in diverse packaging. Now
alcoholics, obsessive-compulsives, kleptomaniacs, and even
schizophrenics are given antidepressants for their underlying
depression. Indeed, some clinicians diagnose depression by a
therapeutic test: If the patient improves after being given antidepressants, he or she must have been depressed. Of course
the cynic may offer the rejoinder that living itself, with its
inevitable mortal outcome, produces an underlying depression.

John Kenneth Galbraith described a similar situation concerning social policy: The remedy prescribes diagnosis. When
we shape diagnosis according to the weapons that are easiest
to use, "diagnosis proceeds from the available remedy." Allowing the availability of remedy to dictate diagnosis "results
in the gross over-simplification of deeply-rooted problems."*
Who can doubt that psychiatry today suffers from the same
malady? What is particularly dangerous here is what almost
amounts to pride in not wanting to know about problems,
deep-rooted or otherwise, in the rush to treat symptoms. This
approach makes a mockery of the meaning of psychiatry itself.

Sanguine in reporting their results (Dr. Kessler's multifaceted approach yields a 70–90 percent improvement), the bio-

* *The Nature of Mass Poverty* (Cambridge: Harvard University Press,
1979), pp. 23–42.

chemical psychiatrists engage in a tautology: The agoraphobic suffers from an underlying depression to be treated with anti-depressants, but about which nothing further is to be said. We are supposed to be reassured that the patient has no interest in uncovering causes or etiology, no desire to think about these matters. It is even suggested by many psychiatrists that the depression itself is endogenous, that there is no outside cause, so it is most probably due to a biochemical imbalance.

The enthusiasm for antidepressants is dampened by a major study by J. B. Morris and A. J. Beck, which showed that only 60 percent of a group of patients found antidepressants superior to placebos.* Taking into account the physical risks involved in the use of powerful drugs and the narrow margin of advantage, placebos should certainly be the treatment of choice. Placebos are inert and harmless and work their wonders as religiously distributed wafers should. The biochemical therapists are undaunted by this disclosure. Loath to believe in pure magic, they now suggest that the placebo is not innocent chemically after all; through its emotional impact (psychosomatic) it triggers the correct biochemical reaction, which in turn becomes curative. Dr. Jon D. Levine suggests that "it is possible that placebos may exert their wide-ranging effects by stimulating any number of natural healing mechanisms in the body, including interferon, which fights viral infections, and steroids, which counter inflammation."** The use of placebos by physicians as well as by psychiatrists is now strongly recommended in many quarters although it is conceded that they work poorly with "chronic complainers." The issue came to the fore in an editorial in the *Journal of the American Medical Association*. Dr. Tomas J. Silber criticized the ethics of their use, the propriety of "fooling the patient."†

Feminist organizations and other groups responding to the damage that historically has been done to women in the name

* "The Efficacy of Anti-depressant Drugs: A Review of Research (1958 to 1972)," *Archives of General Psychiatry*, 30 (1974): 667–74.

** *The New York Times*, April 3, 1979.

† Vol. 242, July 20, 1979, p. 245.

of treatment have focused on the double standards that prevail in medicine, especially in psychiatry where women are drugged and hospitalized (here lobotomized) more often than men. Prefrontal lobotomy was generally used for the most severe, regressed, and untreatable cases of schizophrenia. In Great Britain we find it having been used for agoraphobia, a psychoneurotic condition, clearly a lesser mental disorder and one where the symptoms associated with psychosis are absent. Yet lobotomy was used on a group of twenty-two patients, four of them male, eighteen female.* To be sure, this gross disparity can be explained by the fact that 88 percent of agoraphobics are women, roughly paralleling this statistic. But since the use of this drastic procedure for a psychoneurosis is highly controversial, the suspicion of experimentation mainly on women is there.

At some level, do the (usually) male physicians find it easier to justify severing a woman's brain than a man's? Is she thought to be less in need of the acute perceptive powers generally attributed to prefrontal lobe functioning? Such questions are equally applicable to other psychiatric therapies, such as giving psychotropic (neuroleptic) drugs where irreversible effects may similarly occur. Here the ratio of women to men is two to one.

During the last ten years the treatment of psychiatric disorders has to a large degree taken a turn toward biochemical or medical solutions. Among many groups of psychiatrists today who are treating agoraphobia, the issue is what drug or combination of drugs works best. They seem to have lost interest in cause or meaning and are instead intent on enabling the person to function as she "ought to" again.

The emphasis is on diminishing or eliminating those symptoms that interfere with the societal expectations of a functioning adult. If you were to suggest that the agoraphobic

---

* I. M. Marks, J. L. T. Birley, and M. G. Gelder, "Modified Leucotomy in Severe Agoraphobia: A Controlled Serial Inquiry," *British Journal of Psychiatry*, 112 (August 1966): 757–69.

might have a problem, the reply would be: Of course, she has a problem leaving the house. The possibility that some moral or social statement underlies the behavior is ignored. Deep problems are not to be solved; symptoms are to be dissolved, and in the process psychiatry itself becomes dissolved as a literate specialty, preempted by medicine. Mental symptoms have always been treated with less respect than physical ones.

The conscientious physician generally will not treat symptoms without determining causation. Not so in the new psychiatry, where symptomatic treatment appears to be an end in itself, even though we occasionally still hear "drugs don't solve problems." Similarly, the possible positive value of grief, of suffering, of being dysfunctional, and even of pain is discounted. They have forgotten Hannah Arendt's oft-quoted reflection: "The human condition is such that pain and effort are not just symptoms which can be removed without changing life itself; they are rather the modes in which life itself, together with the necessity to which it is bound, makes itself felt. For mortals, the easy life of the gods would be a lifeless life."

The new mental drugs are potent indeed; they are used in subduing ferocious animals. That they make human beings more docile and cooperative, more manageable, can be seen on any ward of a mental hospital, where drugs have replaced the physical restraints formerly used for disturbed patients. The issue here is ultimately the moral and ethical dilemma of whether these patients, as well as outpatients such as agoraphobics, are disturbed or disturbing. We are on safer ground if we consider them disturbed, else we may be drugging or otherwise restraining them because of our own sensibilities. But this still has consequences for our concept of human rights. Drugs are frequently administered against the patient's will and consent, and often without her knowledge, because we have determined that she is suffering and it is our medical and merciful duty to relieve her panic, anxiety, and/or pain. In judging another's pain, we take on an awesome responsibility. Couldn't we self-servingly misinterpret protest for pain, thus subduing our enemies or adversaries who, we convince ourselves, are in terrible pain? These moral issues often become secondary to therapeutic expediency and, in Ernest Becker's idiom, signify the "death of meaning."

It is the rare agoraphobic who has not been medicated for her illness. The exceptions tend to be those in psychotherapy or psychoanalysis, but even here the combination of drugs and psychotherapy is often tried. Freud himself at one time justified the use of extra-analytic intrusions, especially in agoraphobic patients. He was known to bend the psychoanalytic rules when the therapy itself seemed in danger of being discontinued if the patient were not given some accommodation. He warned, however, that the intrusion should be short-lived and the subject of intense discussion thereafter. The prohibition against the use of drugs, especially in agoraphobic patients, is based on the logical proposition that the patient should not be distracted from the "work" of therapy, and what might sound strange to our pragmatists, that the patient should not experience relief through deception, false assurance, or coercion, all of which are known to bring quick, if temporary, relief. Similarly, relief should not come from the charisma or authority of the therapist via a placebo effect. The hope is that relief will come through personal psychological and social mastery, without having to attribute the "cure" to magic or medicine. If the latter, it is a sad note in the new biochemical psychiatry that there is little mention of what happens to a patient's self-confidence, feelings of self-worth, or pride in mastery when she perceives, and it is abundantly indicated to her, that her newfound confidence or ability to proceed is a result of drugs. With all its purported shortcomings, psychoanalysis attempts to "strengthen the ego." Drug therapies achieve the opposite by fostering dependence, habituation, even addiction, but worst of all, undermine confidence in the self as capable of mastery. Much as psychiatric biochemists obfuscate the difference, mastery over a psychological, social, or interpersonal problem or conflict is in no way the same as overcoming pneumonia or scurvy.

According to Donald Klein, patients seem to experience tremendous stimulation from small doses of the drugs used for treatment. This is the proper treatment "because these patients experience a complete blockade of their panic attacks on homeopathic levels of the drug." The patient is started on small doses, which can be increased if "stimulation" is not developed. Physicians generally question both the efficacy and the medical validity of homeopathic doses. They are suspicious of the "placebo effect."

Klein fails to explain why antidepressants ("uppers") are so helpful, other than that they "treat" the panic. As in many other psychiatric conditions, when the agoraphobic on uppers expresses euphoria or even appears to brighten up, an "underlying depression" is retrospectively diagnosed. This justification and rationalization of mood elevators is now found everywhere in the psychiatric literature.

In the same vein is the incongruity of attempting to reason together with a person, as one does in psychotherapy, while one is administering drugs. The physician-therapist then has it within his power to grant or withhold his bag of goodies as the spirit moves him. In the rush to test the clinical efficacy of this or that drug, the ethics of donor-recipient interaction has been ignored. Power plays are an inherent risk in any psychiatric relationship; here the risks are that much greater. And in the process the human spirit loses its importance.

Biochemical psychiatrist Donald Klein feels that the therapy for the agoraphobic woman should be directed toward her panic attacks rather than her anxiety. Therapies directed toward curing the latter are doomed to failure. Klein claims that sedatives, such as barbiturates and alcohol, may be deleterious to the patient. Similarly, phenothiazene, which may be beneficial for psychotic anxiety, fails here and may have a demoralizing effect. There is also the danger that she may become an addict or an alcoholic. He recommends antidepressants, Tofranil in particular.

As far as cause or etiology of agoraphobia is concerned, Klein does not equivocate: "Panic attacks are the root cause of the condition." He continues: "The first of the panic attacks usually occurs suddenly. The patient probably felt good before the attack." What does Klein mean by "felt good"? In good health? Felt good about her life, her job, etc.? These issues do not enter the domain of inquiry for biochemical psychiatry. And why should they, if tiny doses of the right chemical make everything good again?

Psychiatrists Lynda Howlett and Richard Markoff, reporting four cases of agoraphobia, three women and one man, similarly found that imipramine (Tofranil) brought relief from panic that was unaffected by other psychotropic drugs. While the acute episode appeared to be relieved by the drug, the chronic anticipatory anxiety from which the patients also suffered was resistant to the treatment.

Here the evidence for efficacy of the therapy is "anecdotal," but apart from four psychotherapy sessions given to one patient for dealing with interpersonal problems, the psychiatrists did not inquire into the life situations of the patients, nor did they wonder about the prevalence of female agoraphobics.

Following Klein's tautological hypotheses that the cause of agoraphobia is panic, British investigators Julian Hafner and Frank Milton, using drugs called beta blockers, are less sanguine about curing panic. Beta blockers are drugs that purportedly block the effects of anxiety or/and panic in those organs that may manifest such reactions. For instance, severe heart palpitations are the most prominent and perhaps most feared reaction. Beta blockers would prevent palpitations. Hafner and Milton gave this drug to twenty-five participants, twenty-two of whom were women. Another group of twenty-five was given a placebo. Both groups functioned better after four weeks of the medication, but the placebo group coped better with panic and was able to travel alone sooner than those on the drug, propranolol (Inderal, Inderide). Their explanation for this seemingly paradoxical reaction was that the group on the drug, no longer experiencing the full measure of panic, was no longer as able to cope with it, whereas the people on placebo, having experienced repeatedly the full impact of panic (somatic manifestations, heart palpitations, etc.), learned to master their fears, apparently building confidence in their own (ego) coping mechanisms. Apparently those who were drugged lost confidence in themselves and became even more fearful. Hafner and Milton wrote: "It is almost inescapable that propranolol influenced the patients' experience of exposure 'in vivo' in a way which adversely affected their subsequent progress."*

* "The Influence of Propranolol on the Exposure *In Vivo* of Agoraphobics," *Psychological Medicine* 7, (1977): 419.

12

The Strikebreakers II: Behaviorists

The behaviorists have a full complement of engineering and manipulative terms, such as implosion, flooding, reciprocal inhibition, and desensitization. Undaunted by the inherent structural complexities of human problems and conflicts, their linear approach toward symptoms parallels that of the biochemists. As their name suggests, they are interested in how people behave. They are not reluctant to assume that they know how people should behave, and go about their business of reformation. Behaviorists don't worry about subtleties, "metapsychology," or deep motives. They find their work rewarding and nearly always report success when others fail. Their results are similarly long-lasting, with no adverse side effects. Their reported cures contain the statement "and there were no symptom-substitutions as the suspicious and doubting psychoanalysts predict about such superficial methods." In those rare instances where the behavior therapy does not succeed it is said that failure is due to the entrenched nature of the behavior pattern and that therapy was started too late in the patient's life.

From the country that gave us Newton and Darwin, Shakespeare and Mill, we read a report by M. G. Gelder and I. M. Marks that desensitization (the patient is taught to relax while slowly reentering the phobic situation, and anxiety is kept to a minimum at all times) had a rapid and rather specific effect on phobic symptoms and, in additon, was followed by improved social adjustment. This is in sharp contrast to the slow pace and "ambiguous" results of individual psychotherapy.

The individual who came under special scrutiny was a twenty-nine-year-old woman who for six years had been afraid to travel in "lifts, planes, and tube trains," in addition to having severe marital problems that led to recurrent separations and depression. Desensitization occurred once a week; she had thirteen sessions "in imagination" and carried out graduated tasks between sessions. After each desensitization treatment there was an immediate improvement on the phobia, and despite some losses between sessions the improvement accumulated gradually week after week. The therapists conclude that desensitization has a specific, salutary effect on phobic symptoms. They warn, however, that it is most effective when the patient does not also have "social problems or personality difficulties."*

J. P. Watson, R. Gaind, and I. M. Marks similarly present "a rapid treatment" in which adults with longstanding phobias are given prolonged continuous exposure to their phobic objects. First the patients listen to tape recordings of the sounds of the feared objects. Then the actual phobic object is presented and the patient is encouraged to approach it as closely as possible and remain in contact with it until the anxiety diminishes. The practice sessions were designed to accommodate the peculiarities of the individual phobias. For the person who feared balloons, ninety were blown up and burst; many feathers were presented to two patients with feather phobias; three patients who feared spiders were exposed to an assortment of spiders; one who feared birds first handled a stuffed one and then was encouraged to touch and play with a pet budgerigar. One patient feared water. She was encouraged to submerge her head in a bowl and later in a bath. And, for the patient who feared thunder, because the feared object ob-

* "Desensitization and Phobias: A Cross-over Study," *British Journal of Psychiatry*, 114 (March 1968): 323–28.

viously could not be produced at will, records of thunder, rain, and wind were played. Patients received two or three sessions, the average total treatment being between four and five hours.

Watson, Gaind, and Marks report that all the patients were greatly helped by the treatment and clinical improvement was maintained at the followup; patients showed little residual fear or avoidance of other phobic objects. They conclude that this method produces better results in less time than other treatments, including desensitization.*

I. Hand, Y. Lamontague, and I. M. Marks have worked with chronic agoraphobic patients. They show the value of "group exposure" or "flooding" (it is also called "implosion"). In flooding, the patient is asked to enter the worst possible phobic situation and to experience the fear at maximum intensity for up to an hour until he or she no longer experiences fear. The procedure is done first in the imagination and then in real life.

Twenty-five agoraphobics were treated this way. The patients were required to proceed alone for up to forty-five minutes into their two most frightening situations. They were to continue treatment exercises beyond the treatment period until nonphobic behavior became an "easy" habit. Divided into groups, all were improved on phobic scales three days after treatment. Group exposure produced unexpected additional gains in social skills and assertion, which were reflected in improved work and leisure activities as well as in social adjustment. However, some patients who had pretreatment marital or personality problems showed exacerbation of these problems during followup. (Such difficulties do occasionally arise during or following therapy.) Apparently the human factors have to be taken into consideration although, as most of the scientific reports indicate, they seldom have any determinative significance.

Despite this occurrence, the behaviorists conclude that ag-

* "Prolonged Exposure: A Rapid Treatment for Phobias," *British Medical Journal* (January 2, 1971): 13–15.

oraphobics can be treated effectively by group exposure in vivo and that group cohesion facilitates treatment and promotes greater improvement after six months.*

The behavior of behaviorists in promoting their skills often offends the sensibilities of both professionals and the informed laity. They compare their results with those of others and in most instances they prevail as the more successful. They have no timidity about exhibiting this self-judged superiority to the public.

Dr. Alan J. Goldstein, a behaviorist and psychologist and the director of the agoraphobic treatment and research center at Temple University, spoke of his work, calling agoraphobics' problem "the fear of fear." They fear going forth into the world because of a mysterious panic that overtakes them, seemingly unrelated to what is going on in their lives.

According to Dr. Goldstein, his treatment "succeeds," even with patients who have spent years and thousands of dollars on other treatments that have "failed." "The traditional one-to-one psychiatric therapies just don't work. They're useless in dealing with agoraphobics." He gives an example: "Let's call her Diane. She is in her early 30's (a classic time for women to contract the problem), very stylish, attractive, and articulate. Diane is married, lives in Northeast Philadelphia, and works as a medical technician to a physician. She was in psychiatric analysis for eight years at a total cost of $10,000. She also visited two other psychiatrists and a hypnotist. She tried to explain the fears that overwhelmed her while driving but her analyst kept plunging her deeper and deeper into her childhood. Finally, Diane became housebound by panic attacks."**

Diane's road to recovery came after she read about agoraphobia in a newspaper. She called the clinic at Temple where

* "Group Exposure (Flooding) *In Vivo* for Agoraphobics," *British Journal of Psychiatry*, 124 (June 1974): 588–602.

** Interview by Mark McGrath, *Temple Alumni Review*, Spring 1979.

she came under the direction of Alan and Susan Jasin. It took them just four months to get her to drive alone on Roosevelt Boulevard. After nearly panicking, she succeeded. Diane describes this as the peak moment of her life.

The Temple University agoraphobic treatment and research program provides each client with red rubber bands to be worn on their wrists and vigorously snapped every time a panic attack is anticipated. The client is warned further that her wrists will be bruised by the end of the week—but never mind, "the rubber band can be your best friend when you are in trouble."

Given the subjectivity of the psychotherapeutic process, along with the vagaries of positive and negative feelings that emerge therefrom, and especially in an area of endeavor as subjective as this, Dr. Goldstein should feel self-conscious about announcing his own successes and others' failures. To say that agoraphobics are really suffering from a "fear of fear" is sadly consistent with general behaviorist belief. These patients supposedly have nothing to fear but fear itself.

Treating symptoms leads to the trivialization of human problems and the people (women) who have them. The oppressed, the powerless have always been dealt with this way, a grand distraction, albeit initiated by patients themselves and returned in spades. It is as if the Grand Inquisitors are saying, "You are complaining about spiders or thunder or streets. We will take you at your word. You surely can have no complaints that we are indifferent to your appeals. We are giving you treatment and cures for your suffering." But the cures and treatment give a message of mindlessness that makes a mockery of the people and their problems. It is difficult to see how people, especially those who have suffered powerlessness, ridicule, and chronic oppression, would ever seriously submit themselves to such indignities.

Two brands of medical treatment were practiced in ancient Greece, one for the citizens, the other for the slaves. Predictably, the masters were given knowledge and information and were educated about their difficulties while the slaves were treated silently. There were two classes of doctors: the "slave-doctor" and the "scientifically trained physician who treats free men."

Werner Jaeger writes: "In *The Laws* Plato gives an amusing description of the difference between the slave-doctor and the scientifically trained doctor who treats free men. He says it consists in their attitude to their patients. The slave-doctor hurries from bed to bed, giving out prescriptions and orders without discussion, i.e., without explaining his treatment, simply working on routine and previous experience. He is an absolute tyrant. If he heard a free doctor talking to free patients in a manner very like scientific instruction, and defining the organs of the disease by going back to the nature of all bodies, he would laugh heartily and say what most so-called doctors retort in such cases: 'You fool, you are not curing your patient, you are *educating* him as if you wanted not to make him healthy, but to make him into a doctor.' But Plato believes that that same medical method which depends on a fundamental education of the patient is the ideal of scientific healing.*

The accusation of educating the patient rather than curing him is heard today against the uncovering, analytical therapies, the therapies that assume some intellect or ideology in the production of the so-called emotionally disturbed. They are to be taken beyond their symptoms, which they dutifully report, especially those who have come to expect no intellectual dialogue from men in authority.

This is knowing your place; it prevents the specter of rejection if you veer from the assigned scenario of responses. As you provide the symptoms, the expert will deal with each one as presented, with no nonsense of wasteful, luxurious educating. Expecting to be educated rather than cured would indicate a hidden desire to aspire to levels beyond your station. This is why so many people of inferior status and power seek out and even cooperate with therapies that so obviously demean and denigrate, and conversely fear those that offer a modicum of respect and intelligence.

* *Paideia: The Ideals of Greek Culture* (New York: Oxford University Press, 1945), vol. 3, p. 12.

Woman have long been in this position, succumbing to inferior offerings to assure the world that they know their place. This is slave psychology, one of the burdens that the oppressed bear. It is the internalization of inferiority that then becomes part of the self and may be deemed a virtue. It engenders a satisfaction and even a desire for things inferior, "things" that in the idiom of psychology become "ego syntonic," at the same time those elements of our civilization of high value become "ego alien" or "ego dystonic," and are treated with the fear and disdain that chronically oppressed people have of intellectuality and science.

It is ironic that just when it begins to be possible for women, because of increasing economic and social power, to get first-class medical treatment, a nostalgia appears, a nostalgia for the irrational, the instinctive, the magical. Our culture in general is embracing mysticism. We read everywhere that vitamins cure cancer, that chants can put a fatal disease into remission, that eating right can give one eternal life.

The feminist culture has not been removed from this foolishness. It is understandable that human beings, given our frailty, our inability to understand so many things, and our mortality, would embrace intuiton. It is further understandable that women, having even less power to control life than men, would do so. Understandable, but not defensible. The only proper answer for people who have little power is to try to get more.

Many women who are respected in the feminist community believe (as does the antifeminist community) that the biological difference between the sexes is of enormous significance. Jane Alpert exalts Mother Right:

> The unique consciousness or sensibility of women, the particular attributes that set feminist art apart, and a compelling line of reseach now being pursued by feminist anthropologists all point to the idea that *female biology is the basis of women's powers*. Biology is hence the source and not the enemy of feminist revolution.

. . . The power of the new feminist culture, the powers
which were attributed to the ancient matriarchies (considered
either as historical fact or as mythic archetypes), and the inner
power with which many women are beginning to feel in touch
and which is the soul of feminist art, may all arise from the
same source. That source is none other than female biology:
the *capacity* to bear and nurture children.

Lest women who are not mothers feel left out of the special
powers category, she assures: "Motherhood must be understood here as a potential which is imprinted in the genes of
every woman; as such it makes no difference to this analysis of
femaleness whether a woman ever has borne, or ever will
bear, a child."*

It is one thing for the oppressor to say the uterus determines the life of women; for the oppressed to agree is too
much to bear. It is interesting to note where this has led and is
leading many women. If we read women's movement literature from throughout this country (indeed from Europe also),
we are struck by the vast amount of time, space, and effort
spent on health foods, exercise information, spiritualism. Different in content perhaps, but not different in form from their
mothers' concerns: food, diet, church.

The anti-intellectual trend is more than boring; it is antipo-
litical. Emphasis on tarot cards, or health through massage
(instead of finding the cause of the stress), keeps women effectively busy and not attending to changes in our political and
economic systems.

Women, who have been relegated to the mindless activities since the beginning of time, are now offered some of the
following, in the name of women's *liberation:*

A workshop on love of the self: We will study the mind
(one mind scientifically studied is the key to all minds) and
share life and death experiences to gain greater understand-

* "Mother Right: A New Feminist Theory," *Ms.*, August 1973, p. 52.

ing of the real nature of Self. Bring blankets, pillows or shawls for meditation.

Women and food: We'll talk about the connection between learning to control the quantity and quality of food we take into our bodies and taking charge of the rest of our lives.

As part of the antirational movement, women are not only being advised to forget the advances of medical science, they are being advised that there is some special kind of "women's law" (read inferior). One women's center writes its subscribers: "Women call because they don't understand what their lawyers tell them . . . . They need emotional support . . . . My experience with advocacy has been that more than anything a woman needs someone she can trust, an arm around her, just to know someone cares." That woman would be better cared for if someone explained to her what the lawyer had said, what ramifications it would have on her life. A big hug is fun, but not what one needs when confronting the legal system in the United States.

What does this have to do with agoraphobia, and the kinds of treatment women are receiving? Women have been trained to expect slave medicine for centuries; and women are being lulled into believing, even by some branches of the women's movement, that nonsense, not sense, is the way to analyze problems. So it is easy for the purveyors of behavior modification to sell their cures to women.

An example of this was found in *Ms.* magazine in an article entitled "Afraid to Leave the House? You May Have Agoraphobia."* Unlike conventional descriptions of the subject, the essay showed ideological insights that were both refreshing and encouraging. For instance, it revealed that most of "the victims are women and 89 percent of all victims are married." The authors correctly comment: "This overbalance clearly reflects the political reality of isolation, powerlessness, and poor self-image that affect women in general."

* Carolyn Kott Washburne and Dianne L. Chambless, *Ms.*, September 1978.

After a cogent analysis, the authors recommend Phobia Clinics, now spread across the country, which focus primarily on behavior therapy and whose practitioners by their own admission (and pridefully so) take an anti-ideological posture as their method of cure. Again, the symptoms are attacked so the cripples can be freed of their disabling inhibitions, ostensibly free to enter the streets, shops, and beauty parlors. Predictably, consistent with most behaviorists' reports of cures and improvements, "80 percent of the women who complete their program, which has been in operation for six years, improve and remain improved."

These results have not been confirmed by others. Yet the *Ms.* article not only recommends behavior therapy as the only therapy that really works, but supplies its readers with the name of behaviorist psychologist Alan Goldstein who "has a referral list of treatment facilities for agoraphobics. For help in locating a phobic clinic near you, contact him by writing to the Behavior Therapy Unit, Temple Department of Psychiatry." (Parenthetically, one of the authors, Chambless, is on the staff of the Behavior Therapy Unit of Temple University.) By any standard, this was a bad day for *Ms.* and for liberators.

At an early stage some gay people became interested in behaviorism as a help for their "problems," until they learned that it was being used in prisons and mental institutions to "normalize" them. Those who willingly submitted to behavior modification—that is, those not ordered to do so by the courts—apparently had internalized the disparagement of themselves and accepted not only humiliation but an instrument for their own undoing. What the gay community has learned, women will also. As their consciousness is raised the popping of both pills and balloons will be identified for what they are.

Another tool of the behaviorists is "social reinforcement." Stewart Agras, Harold Leitenberg, and David Barlow studied three cases of agoraphobia (two women and one man) to test the efficacy of this technique in modifying neurotic behavior in human beings, as had been successfully accomplished to "control normal animal and human behavior in the laboratory."*

The subjects were sequentially given the reinforcement; then it was withdrawn. The change in their progress or decline in performance was observed. The patients were asked to walk certain distances alone away from "the dependent situation," in this case the Clinical Research Center. The social reinforcement consisted of being praised when they did well, as the attempt was made and as the distances increased. The control consisted of withdrawing praise for the same activity, keeping all other circumstances the same. Specifically, the social reinforcement came from the therapist and others at the clinic saying "Good . . . you're doing well" with appropriate enthusiasm. Also during the reinforcement phase, remarks made by the patient to the nursing staff about progress were praised. They found that with praise the patients did well but when the reinforcement was withdrawn there was either no further improvement or a decline. On the other hand, reinstatement of reinforcement led to a rapid reacquisition of the lost behavior in each subject. This, along with other reactions, the investigators reassure us, parallels behavior found in laboratory animals.**

There is something stomach-turning about treating a fellow human being this way, even in the name of scientific investigation, or with the license that seems to come automatically when one labels another "neurotic." In dealing with adult human beings in trouble, "social reinforcement" might instead take on dimensions such as eliminating sex discrimination in hiring, equal pay for equal work, making the marriage contract more equitable, aiding in the development of talents and skills, and offering other educational opportunities. These are the social reinforcements that may have real significance for a thinking, striving person. But Agras, Leitenberg, and Barlow have little patience with such sentiments:

* "Social Reinforcement in the Modification of Agoraphobia," *Archives of General Psychiatry*, 19 (October 1968): 423–27.
** Ibid., pp. 425–27.

"The common assumption that neurotic behavior cannot be modified by variables that have been shown to control normal animal and human behavior in the laboratory, seem to have little basis in fact."* We are left wondering what variable that has been shown to control normal animal behavior in the laboratory could account for Emily Dickinson's poetry.

The great pride of the civilized world is that we strive not to treat people like animals. Mary Baker Eddy scolded Phineas Quimby because he claimed his power of cure came from "animal" magnetism. She insisted that more transcendent forces were involved. What a fine day in the history of behavioral science it would be if leading behaviorists (and psychiatric biochemists) declared: "These techniques of control are contraindicated *because* they have been found to work on laboratory animals."**

Dr. Julian Hafner, a British behaviorist, feels the spouse is important in determing the outcome of "intensive behavioral" treatment. He quotes with apparent approval the insistence by Webster (another behaviorist) on the involvement in therapy of the spouse: "Only those patients whose husbands came for treatment showed any degree of improvement. The point cannot be overemphasized that the husband is the therapist's only means of entrance into a closed and self-sustaining system."

Hafner's study begins with an operational definition of agoraphobia: "The inability or reluctance to leave home, or to enter public places or schools, alone or accompanied, because of anxiety or other unpleasant symptoms, or a fear of falling, fainting or otherwise losing control." He adds that most of the women selected had a "range of general neurotic and phobic symptoms in addition to their agoraphobia." The mean duration of the agoraphobia was 9.5 years; the duration of the marriage, 12.7 years. Thirty-three women participated in the

---

* Ibid., pp. 426–27.
** For a critical exposition of psychology laboratory antics, see Morton Hunt, "Research Through Deception," *New York Times Magazine* (September 12, 1982).

study. Husbands were asked to accompany their wives on all visits except those during treatment itself. The treatment consisted of exposure in real life to feared situations. The husbands were asked to cooperate in the patients' post-treatment programs. Both patients and husbands were given a battery of questions designed mainly to quantify "hostility" in the various groups. A paradoxical reaction was uncovered: A proportion of the husbands were adversely affected by their wives' initial symptomatic improvement, but they "improved when their wives partially relapsed."

Hafner relates that one husband in the most hostile group attempted suicide about four months after the treatment. He said that he did so because "since his wife's recovery he had felt useless and inadequate." He lamented that she was no longer as dependent on him as she had been while agoraphobic. Four husbands became depressed when the "focus of dissatisfaction" within their marriage shifted back from their wives' problems to their own sexual difficulties. In four others (including the one who attempted suicide), their wives' recovery revealed abnormal jealousy that was dormant as long as the wives were unable to go out alone. Wives, in turn, tried to deal with this marital disharmony by partially resuming their agoraphobic behavior.

Hafner was impressed with the husbands' universal denial of their own problems: "These men . . . were able to acknowledge their difficulties only after developing a supporting and non-threatening relationship with the author in the context of repeated follow up visits ostensibly for their wives' benefit." Hafner concludes: "Any study aimed at understanding phobia disorders in married females which fails to acknowledge the importance of denial in their husbands seems unlikely to be fully successful." His study supports the thesis that married women who are agoraphobic are unlikely to relinquish their symptoms unless their husbands enter appropriate psychiatric treatment.*

* "Agoraphobic Women Married to Abnormally Jealous Men," *British Journal of Medical Psychology*, 52 (June 1979): 99–104.

Hafner's work indicates that there is some hope for behaviorists. He does see, albeit ingenuously, an interpersonal dynamic to "this madness," that agoraphobia is not simply a bad habit, or a fear of fear, unrelated to life situations. However, his treatment naively follows the pattern of curing through exposure to the purported danger, as if the danger were out on the street, rather than, as he belatedly discovered, in the home. (Sartre could have told him: "Hell is the other person.") He says nothing about marriage and its expectations, as if this were an issue apart from what was going on between his patients and their husbands. Instead he promotes the villain theory, finding the hapless husband to blame. The woman supposedly succumbs to his hostility, for which the husband must be treated. What an escape clause for behaviorist failures: How do you expect us to cure you when your husband kicks and screams or otherwise falls apart whenever you improve? Despite his acknowledgment of the adversarial and even antagonistic elements in these marriages, Hafner seems oblivious to the inherent dangers in seeing husbands and wives separately and together, in therapy or consultation. He doesn't consider such issues as permission, privacy, confidentiality, conflicts of interest. Perhaps some of the husbands' hostility was as much in response to Hafner's roughshod intrusion as to the wives' illness.

13

The Strikebreakers III: Pipe Dreams
to Pipe Cleaners

Sleep as therapy, as something curative and reparative, has a tradition as old as our civilization itself. Shakespeare called it the "balm of hurt minds." The ancient Greeks placed great faith in what they called "the Temple" sleep, or incubation. The suppliant (patient) inhaled aromatic herbs, "which brought on a light stupor, conducive to dreams and apparitions." He slept on the skin of the victim he had sacrificed, a ceremony designed to increase the tendency to dream and to enhance clarity of vision. The dreams were then related to priests, who provided the appropriate interpretations. The suppliant might remain there from twelve hours to four months.*

Throughout the years, putting "troubled" people to sleep has lost none of its appeal and mystery. Whether it does any good is still unresolved. And it is not clear who is the beneficiary, the person involved or the people around him who are at least temporarily relieved of his disturbing presence. "Putting to sleep" has an ominous side, often being a euphemism for "putting to death." And death in general is referred to as

---

* D. Kouretas, "A Chapter of Psychosomatic Medicine: The Practice of Therapy in the Temple of Amphiaraos," *Medical Annals*, 6 (August 1966): 679–93.

"the eternal sleep or slumber" by poets and religionists who give hope to our fantasies of immortality. It can also serve as an accusation of irresponsibility: The responsible person should remain awake and alert to deal with the problems at hand. Only the obstructive and unhelpful are typically sedated to keep them out of the way so that others may be efficiently active and productive.

The need to absolve ourselves of guilt for removing others has been a prime factor in promoting the disease concept with regard to human behavior. Agoraphobia is no exception. Everything becomes focused on the "afflicted" person. Here, too, is the suspicion that her behavior is as upsetting to those around as it is to her. Her behavior upsets the smooth operation of the household and family. Minimally she must attempt to do something about it. This she seeks to do, which explains the never-ending stream of opportunist therapists who present themselves with cures. It is inevitable that she would be put to sleep.

A preliminary report of "sleep treatment" explained the rationale for using the hypnotic thiopentone for the relief of "tension and depersonalization" in phobic patients. (This therapy was adopted from the Pentothal Abreaction therapy used extensively during World War II and later to a limited degree in civilian practice.) The patient is put to sleep by the slow injection of the drug and is given simple explanations and reassurance during the stage of induction. It is performed on alternate days, usually three times a week, until improvement is noted. The first series consisted of thirty-two patients, many of whom were "chronically ill." The results were "outstanding." Sixteen became largely or wholly symptom-free and nine were improved after a course of treatment. One woman who had been completely housebound and oppressed by feelings of depression for ten years lost her symptoms and resumed a perfectly normal life. Although complete recovery is admittedly rare, "in many patients the symptoms became mild, fleeting and infrequent," the "change had a qualitative stamp and their lives were transformed by it."

Although the investigators caution about the difficulty in assessing the value of a new treatment of neurosis, the figure of 85 percent improvement had to be considered encouraging and impressive, particularly in a condition that generally resisted other treatments. Furthermore, the inventors speculate that their salutary results with this chemical (physical) treatment might well be fruitful in identifying the causes of neurotic illness.*

Nothing more has been heard about this most successful therapy although the use of chemistry in psychiatry is increasing. However, if the results of this preliminary report were authentic or could be repeated, the problem of agoraphobia would have been wiped out like smallpox. Instead, at least a dozen other therapies have surfaced.

Eidetic imagery therapy for agoraphobia is described by its inventors, Dr. Anne T. Dolan and Anees A. Sheikh, as a short-term approach distinguished from the behavioristic because it goes beyond the symptoms to original causes, and from psychoanalysis because "it does not push the question too far back into the remote and dormant areas of conflict." Thus it cannot be accused of the simplemindedness of the former and the cumbersome complexities of the latter. It can provide a flexible and successful treatment of the symptom, not through tomfoolery, but through understanding, as the angels would have it. The method is complex and based on the therapist's actively digging out significant events of the person's life, present and past, that may have caused the symptom. It is symptom-oriented, based on individual traumatic events, using the theory that connecting symptom and trauma will bring salutary results. The therapy is not interested in extraneous matters that only "prolong the agony" and are irrelevant any-

* Martin Roth, "Phobic Anxiety-depersonalization Syndrome" (abridged), *The Proceedings of the Royal Academy of Medicine*, 52 (1959): 587; Arthur King and J. Crawford Little, "Thiopentone Treatment of the Phobic Anxiety-depersonalization Syndrome, A Preliminary Report" (abridged), *The Proceedings of the Royal Academy of Medicine*, 52 (1959): 595.

way. It is the medical model all over again—excising the malignant tissue.

The inventors describe five stages of the eidetic method: (1) Initial exploration, consisting of history taking. The complaint is investigated to determine whether it appears as an isolated image, somatic response, or meaning (ISM). (2) The Introduction to Eidetics. In the practice session the patient is asked to recall any recent experiences and to visualize them in the form of an image, with the expectation that in future sessions she will see images of this type. (3) Composing the symptom. The offending symptom is dealt with as a visual image, and the therapist takes note of the patient's area of concern about the symptom. (4) Age Projection Test. The therapist asks the various names by which the patient has been known since childhood, suggesting certain words to which the patient will respond by seeing an image of herself in the past. The salient features of the symptoms are repeated, at which time the patient is addressed by her various names alternately. This repetition artificially activates the symptom "to an unbearable acuteness." Suddenly the therapist pulls the carpet on the patient by talking about times when she was healthy and happy in those areas where the symptom now exists. The patient thereupon forms a self-image, is asked to describe it, the place where it appears, and the events occurring prior to, during, and following the age projected in the self-image. This procedure successfully produces recollections of significant events connected with the phobias. (5) The last stage of the therapy is called Study of the Precipitating Event. When the significant eidetic is located and the patient concentrates on it, the full-blown symptom manifests itself. Thereafter, through the repetition of the positive and negative poles of the eidetic, the meaning of the symptom becomes spontaneously clearer and a deep psychodynamic interpretation of the material takes place.*

This "successful treatment" is based on the abreactive

* "Short-term Treatment of Phobia Through Eidetic Imagery," *American Journal of Psychotherapy*, 31 (October 1977): 595–604.

model of cure in which the patient becomes "normal" after regressing to the scene of the crime (trauma), painfully reliving it with full emotion, and extruding it forever from her system like an obstructive foreign body. In the eidetic concept the patient seemingly activates her own internal home horror movies and then screams and cringes as if watching Dracula. Whether called eidetic, emotive, or abreactive, it was part of that naive approach (very early Freud) that hoped for quick and easy solutions—being "repaired" by "getting it out of your system." It is attractive to those therapists and patients who don't want to know about, much less face, the ongoing worldly forces that did and do determine what we are, including our foibles and phobias. In addition, being directed inward and backward relieves us of the responsibilities and agonies of becoming active and making significant changes.

Paradoxical intention or logotherapy was used by Dr. Hans O. Gerz for phobic as well as obsessive-compulsive patients. (This technique was originally devised by Viktor E. Frankl.) Dr. Gerz reports on seven of his twenty-four cases, whom he treated successfully over a four-year period.*

His report begins with the now almost routine prologue stating that psychoanalytically oriented psychotherapy has had little success in this area in contrast to his own, which, predictably, does very well.

He describes the typical anticipatory anxiety of the phobic and reasons that the more the phobic patient fears the occurrence of the symptom and the more she tries to avoid it, the more likely it is to occur. For example, the patient who has a fear of blushing will actually do so as soon as she is afraid that she might and as soon as she tries hard not to. Gerz says, "Suppose we play the game in the opposite way—as to get the recalcitrant child to go to bed: Johnny come here; you must stay up until midnight with Mommy and Daddy watching television." This is what has been called using child psychol-

---

* "The Treatment of the Phobic and the Obsessive-Compulsive Patient Using Paradoxical Intention," *Journal of Neuropsychiatry* 3 (August 1962): 375–87.

ogy. How would it be, then, instead of trying not to blush, if the patient tried to blush; or instead of trying not to pass out, she tried to do so?

Since the autonomic nervous system is outside of conscious control, the patient will not be able to blush or to faint on command. This, however, is the phenomenon used in the technique of paradoxical intention. Instead of being mortally fearful of blushing or fainting, she will be striving to achieve these results. Then, moving from fearing these symptoms to liking them, she will find herself in an amusing situation. She will then, we are told, begin to laugh at her symptoms. Her laughter will somehow strangle the neurotic symptoms.

The more she tries to produce the symptoms, the more incompetent she is to do so. She then becomes responsible for curing herself; this prevents her from becoming dependent on the therapist. The application of paradoxical intention must be repeated again and again because neurotic patterns tend to repeat themselves; they do not easily succumb to new "intentions." In summary, when the patient tries to achieve the involuntary voluntarily, she finally gains control over it (negative practice). Despite the great successes reported by Dr. Gerz, paradoxical intention has not emerged or prevailed as the great cure for agoraphobia, or for that matter, for any of the other phobic or obsessive-compulsive syndromes.

Why can't human beings enjoy something without immediately pondering its medically curative potentials? Thus beer, a legitimate product for fun and frolic, has to be turned into a hair shampoo; electroshock was lifted from an abattoir; lithium, an effective rat poison, becomes a therapy for manic-depressive psychosis. Perhaps the archetype for this compulsive utilitarianism is the sex drive; certainly its efforts, justified by the pleasure it gives, by the design of some great Spirit is alleged to be inextricably tied to the production of something.

It comes as no surprise that that great new international pastime, running, should be promoted for something beyond its immediate pleasure and healthful effects. Yes, running may be a cure for agoraphobia—not the running of one's home or of one's life, but running on the streets as a cure for the fear of walking on the streets.*

Word comes from England that eight patients suffering from agoraphobia have been successfully treated by running, a variant of an older treatment called respiratory relief. Here the relief of simple phobic conditions comes upon breathing after prolonged breath-holding (from an exercise from childhood?). The technique for curing agoraphobia is as follows: After identifying the fearful street or area, the patient is directed to reach it breathless from running and then to walk on or through it until anxiety supervenes.

The patient usually advances by running in a linear fashion away from the base until she enters the "anxiety zone" and is then made to travel as near as possible circumferentially so that she remains a fixed distance and time from the base. A variant of this therapy is to direct the patient to run right through the anxiety zone and to repeat this action at a gradually reduced pace, until she is walking.

The eight agoraphobes were successfully treated in a hospital setting (what are agoraphobes doing in a hospital?) with a minimum of therapeutic time involvement by psychiatrists; with one exception all actual treatment was carried out by nurses. But even the help of a nurse is not essential; in many instances patients successfully treated themselves with the assistance of spouses. If there are relapses, the procedure can easily be repeated by the patient.

Finally, we are given physiological theories involving the autonomic nervous system and metabolic needs for vigorous physical activity.

Contextual analysis therapy was invented by Dr. Manual D. Zane of White Plains, New York. It is used to cure agoraphobics, but Zane feels that it may also "open new scientific

* Arnold Orwin, "The Running Treatment: A Preliminary Communication on a New Use of an Old Therapy (Physical Activity) in the Agoraphobic Syndrome," *British Journal of Psychiatry*, 122 (February 1973): 175–79.

vistas for psychiatry."* Like the behaviorists and biochemists, he too is little concerned about origins, social or psychological forces. He concentrates on the nature of and especially the "changes in form of the disturbed behavior." The attention to change of form is the unique part of his therapy. He modestly admits that he bases his idea on the foundation of all modern science, as when Galileo started to study not the motion of bodies but the changes of motion.

Dr. Zane focuses exclusively on the changes in behavior of the afflicted person as she is confronted by or going through the phobic situation. The presence and reassurance of the therapist are an integral part of the therapy. Dr. Zane is an in vivo interventionist; he goes into elevators and bathrooms as well as on more conventional trips with his patients. His therapy covers all bases. It can be short- or long-term, it can be one-to-one or group. "Cured" patients can be taught to help others. And as indicated above, he believes this theory and therapy may transform all of psychiatry as a new "scientific breakthrough."

Dr. Zane claims special preparation and expertise in this field of changing behavior because of earlier work with the physically handicapped in rehabilitation medicine, where he "learned how to analyze motor behavior directly." This has somehow given him a special understanding of agoraphobics; his training in physical medicine encourages his seeing patients as objects, to be dealt with in arbitrary and authoritarian ways, justified by the promises of healing, cure, and rehabilitation. Working with the physically handicapped is probably the very worst preparation for dealing with the emotional problems that exist in conditions like agoraphobia, for here there is nothing "wrong" with the brain, spinal cord, or limbs of the patient.

Although it is undeniable that there may be an emotional overlay to physical conditions, such problems are overwhelmingly organic in nature. Just the opposite is true, of course, in

* "Contextual Analysis and Treatment of Phobic Behavior as It Changes," *American Journal of Psychotherapy*, 32 (July 1978): 338–55.

agoraphobia. Here all systems are intact, and they function adequately except for the inhibitions, restraints, or prohibitions imposed by will, convictions, ideology, or motivation, be these reasonable or irrational.

Dr. Zane's orientation toward physical medicine explains why he does not give us even the skeleton of a social history of his patients. He presents five cases in some detail. They are Mona, Alicia, Debbie, Norma, and Thomas. In each of the case histories only the horrible incapacitating phobia is described. What the persons do, what they think, what they want in life, whether they are poor or rich, are not part of the new scientific study of change. Dr. Zane relates one case with special pride of accomplishment.

> For ten years Norma had many fears and would not travel outside a four block radius from her apartment in the Bronx. Among other fears, she would not step into an elevator, a bus, a train, or a revolving door, became frantic if her car was blocked in traffic and would not shut her bathroom door. I treated her for almost three years in the actual settings where her phobic behavior arose and changed innumerable times. . . . What I learned and the satisfactions of seeing the patient develop as a creative, industrious and constructive human being were more than adequate reward for my unusual effort.
>
> At our first session in her apartment I suggested we go into her bathroom and try to close the door while her husband waited outside. She immediately said, "No." Her refusal of such a simple task particularly after I explained the value of her confronting her feelings of fear and of learning new ways of responding was almost incredible and a little annoying to me. I asked what caused her to say "No." She said that the moment she thought of closing the door, her heart jumped, she had difficulty breathing, she felt panicky and immediately said, "No." She also added her concern that the lock seemed defective and she would be trapped.
>
> I suggested that we study the workings of the lock. Repeatedly she locked and unlocked the mechanisms successfully. Finally she agreed to step into the bathroom with me and shut the door. The moment the door closed, she immediately

opened it again. She said she had thought and felt it would not open and panicked. I pointed out how automatically she had responded to the remote possibility that the door would not open. She agreed that it was realistically much more probable that it would open. I encouraged her to try again. She then let the door shut. With her consent I then locked the door. Unexpectedly the lock clicked. She jumped but recovered quickly and proceeded to unlock it herself. She repeated the closing and locking operations. Then she agreed for me to step outside. I reminded her that she had managed the door and lock herself. Though very frightened and complaining of palpitations, lightheadedness and chest pressure, she held on to the realities of the task and was able to lock and then open the door herself. Afterwards she spoke of being both very tired and very pleased.*

From England comes an investigation of the possible role of tablet color in the drug treatment of patients with anxiety states. Forty-seven patients were studied, twenty-seven female and twenty male, using the psychotropic drug oxazepam (Serax).* The usual double-blind precautions to ensure objectivity were scrupulously observed, and although "significant improvement" in symptoms of psychic anxiety was reported by patients, the differences between colors—yellow, green, and red—were statistically insignificant. However, all was not lost, for certain interesting trends were observed: All the patients with symptoms of anxiety showed the best response when they took the active preparation in a green color, whereas for patients with depressive symptoms, yellow pills seemed to be the most effective. (Yellow appeared to be the least effective for patients with anxiety symptoms.) The physicians also made ratings from their observations. Their ratings for color closely paralleled those of the patients, although the physicians' appraisal of the effectiveness of green as salutary for the phobias was more positive, reaching statistical significance. We are given no theory to account for the different

* Kurt Schapiro, H. A. McClelland, N. R. Griffiths, and D. J. Newell, "Study on the Effects of Tablet Colour in the Treatment of Anxiety States," *British Medical Journal*, 2 (May 1970): 446–49.

responses, no suggestion as to why green works so well for anxious and phobic patients while depressed patients prefer yellow. (Parenthetically, and editorially, we must add that all the physicians and subjects involved were adults.)

Are physicians to be criticized or ridiculed for wanting best results for their patients? Of course not. The dramatic effects of art and nature may irritate or soothe. We can argue, however, that patients may gravitate toward those colored elements of the world that elicit pleasure (or pain) by themselves, without having them literally thrust down their collective throats.

In the Disney World of therapies, the best show comes from Dr. Claire Weekes, of Sidney, Australia. Whereas behaviorists discuss at great length their methods and the results of "desensitization," Dr. Weekes has invented a therapy called "self-desensitization."* She declares that the agoraphobic must learn to pass through panic and to rid herself of any drug dependency. (The latter goal we can unequivocably cheer, but drug dependency is really the doctor's malady, not the patient's.) Self-desensitization basically consists of facing and performing those activities that one fears without the presence of a companion, aide, or counselor. The patient reassures herself, calling on Dr. Weekes's books, pamphlets, recordings and tapes, which are readily purchasable.

While psychoanalysts and other worriers derive their speculations from 4 to 6 cases at most, Dr. Weekes surveyed 528 agoraphobic men and women. After dismissing "deep conflicts," she concludes that in 90 percent of the cases the precipitating cause of the agoraphobia was stress. Of the remaining, 5 percent could offer no cause, and, what may be a mortal blow to psychoanalysts around the world, only 5 percent complained of sexual problems.

The stresses may be of two kinds: sudden stress (sudden shock to the nervous system) such as an exhausting surgical operation, severe hemorrhage, accident, difficult confinement,

* *Simple, Effective Treatment of Agoraphobia* (New York: Hawthorn Books, 1976).

and great grief; or prolonged, intensifying stress due to a difficult life situation, excessive dieting, severe anemia, recover-
ing from a debilitating illness, and so on.

Dr. Weekes tells us: "I do not spend time searching for
hidden, subconscious causes for agoraphobia, neither am I
perturbed if I can find no specific conscious cause." Not only
that, Dr. Weekes is puzzled that other clinicians believe there
may be *causes* for anxiety.

> I stress again that in the vast majority of my agoraphobic
> patients the cause was neither deep-seated nor difficult to
> find. Their agoraphobia was the result of severe sensitization
> suddenly or gradually acquired and kept alive by bewilder-
> ment and fear.
>
> I have been surprised at the intensity with which some of
> my colleagues have defended their belief that an anxiety state
> is due either to some deep-seated cause (perhaps subcon-
> scious) or to some character inadequacy and that the illness
> can be cured only if such causes are found and treated.
>
> . . . Many therapists would admit the possibility that
> some people have a subconscious cause for their agoraphobia
> and need psychoanalysis. I do not close my mind to this possi-
> bility, but it is interesting that over 30 years of practice and
> after curing many hundreds of agoraphobic people, it was not
> necessary for me to use psychoanalysis on any of my pa-
> tients.*

To promote a simple, effective treatment, it would not do
to spend time searching or to become perturbed. In all fair-
ness to Dr. Weekes, to do so would be very difficult due to the
sheer size of her undertakings. These are her own stated fig-
ures: "During 1966–74, I treated (in addition to patients in
private practice) approximately 2000 agoraphobic men and
women, mainly in the United Kingdom, Canada, and the
United States, by remote direction in the form of two books
(*Peace from Nervous Suffering* and *Hope and Help for Your
Nerves*), an album of two long-laying (*sic*) records (*Hope and
Help for Your Nerves*), cassettes (*Moving Toward Freedom,*

* Ibid., pp. 34–37.

Going on Holiday and *Rising in the Morning and Facing the Day*) for a portable tape recorder, and (1969–75) a quarterly magazine of direction and encouragement."

In her 1970 survey, Weekes found that 91 percent of the agoraphobes were female. Of the 486 women, only 51 were single; of the 42 men, 16 were single. Of the females, 78 percent were full-time housewives, 12 percent were housewives who also worked outside the home part-time, and 10 percent worked full-time away from home. Five percent of the men were retired. She is not concerned why 80 to 90 percent of her patients are housewives. She merely states that a housewife can send a child to do the shopping, or wait until the weekend to shop with her husband, whereas a man is obliged to leave the house daily.

Weekes then describes some men's agoraphobia as the citybound executive syndrome. They avoid traveling to outlying districts and avoid those jobs that mean traveling out of town. All is straightforward, simple, effective. She writes: "Self-desensitization, in my experience, is the only treatment that allows the agoraphobic to face the future with confidence."

According to Dan Rather, Dr. Arthur Hardy "is probably the most experienced specialist in phobias in the country. He's been working at it for seventeen years." His methods have been described and promoted on national television programs and in a wide variety of popular magazines.

On *60 Minutes,* Rather asked Hardy why the incidence of agoraphobia is four women for every one man. Hardy replied: "I don't know. I have a theory about it. I think it's more difficult in this culture to be a woman. And I think more restrictions are placed on women. And then I think, according to my definition, in a way women have a tendency to be more emotional. Now, I'm just talking in general terms."*

What Hardy says about agoraphobia is unobjectionable. He tells people the kinds of things they already know, making them feel comfortable. For example, when asked how agora-

* From transcript of interview of Dr. Arthur Hardy on *60 Minutes,* CBS, July 16, 1978.

phobia starts, he replied:

> Victims can be described as excitable personalities. As
> young children they cry fast, anger quickly and are very affec-
> tionate. I call them closet extroverts. Left alone they'd be fine,
> but parents or teachers or siblings criticize them for their
> open feelings. They are told "There is nothing to cry about,"
> or are scolded when they giggle. This criticism is devastating
> to them.
> . . . They become rule-bound. They do not take charge of
> their lives.*

This description fits almost all children, particularly female children.

The interviewer persists, asking Hardy to explain the high
incidence of women. "I think this is partly because it is easier
for women to ask for help, but also because more pressure is
put on little girls by parents and other authorities to be lady-
like and to conform in dress and appearance. I've always fig-
ured women have a tougher row to hoe than men. However,
when a man suffers from agoraphobia it can be very hard because he so often has to fend for himself and his family.**

These long-suffering persons are not to suffer long once
they contact Hardy, who supervises the treatment of agoraphobia at fifteen centers across the country. He tells *People* about
one success, "a woman who hadn't left her house in seven
years. In 20 minutes [his assistant, an ex-patient, as most of
them are] had her standing at the door. In an hour she was
down the street. In a week she was driving a car and
shopping."

Shopping is important in the Hardy cures. In his booklet,
Agoraphobia: Symptoms, Causes, Treatment, published by
Terrap (his organization), he reports on a dramatic cure:
"Once freed of her fears, Anna did many other things she
hadn't dreamed possible, including blowing $1200 in a de-

---

* *People,* August 7, 1978, pp. 88–90.
** Ibid., p. 89.

partment store in her elation over being able to shop without anxiety" (p. 32).

The Hardy method, like so many others, ignores social and psychological context. This omission is not accidental; it is part of the credo: "All at Terrap help conduct the rap sessions and provide direction, guidance, and information about the problem of phobias. The emphasis is strictly on action and progress. We allow no story telling and very little insight searching. Rather we concentrate on progress reports and methods used to obtain progress" (p. 39).

Hardy encourages "getting in touch with yourself" but discourages thinking. When he appeared on the *Phil Donahue Show*, a woman in the audience reported that she had been a flight attendant before her marriage, and had in the course of her duties experienced many hazardous adventures in the air, all without panic. When she married she quit her job. En route to her honeymoon she experienced terrible panic on the airplane, and has been unable to fly ever since. Hardy demonstrated on the air certain methods this woman could use to solve her problem. But he did not mention that she had quit her job to become a full-time wife. This factor must be significant in trying to figure out why a former flight attendant suddenly panics on an airplane.

Hardy believes that a phobia is a learned habit that can be broken through the use of two techniques: relaxation and desensitization; and the corrective emotional experience, or gradual exposure to noxious stimuli (exposure therapy).

In the relaxation method, the person gets into a comfortable position, loosens tight clothing, takes a deep breath, and starts to relax. This method gives "moderate to marked improvement" in 80 to 90 percent of the clients. Exposure therapy requires from ten to twenty hours of practice, under expert guidance, and "results in a significant drop in felt anxiety in the chosen situation and situations similar to it."

Hardy provides gainful careers for his followers and surely that is good therapy. He says of his cured clients, "It is strictly self-help. I put the tools in their hands, but they have to do it themselves."

Dr. Monte J. Meldman of the Chicago Medical School and director of research at Forest Hospital, Des Plaines, Illinois, has come up with another therapy for agoraphobia, and in so doing has found another use for pipe cleaners. There is something in the practical Western mentality that likes to find many uses for things we have around the house. Using them to make wire dolls never became a profitable art form.

Dr. Meldman reports that he has invented the "attention antenna," a pipe cleaner that attaches to the patient's eyeglasses and protrudes vertically about three inches in front of the lens. This enables agoraphobics to overcome their fear of open spaces: Because the antenna is attached to the stem of the patient's glasses, it always appears in the same place in the vision field and provides a constant point of reference. This effectively reduces the dizziness and anxiety that agoraphobics usually experience because of their purported inability to "synthesize visual stimuli into a coherent figure-ground pattern."

The four agoraphobic patients on whom it was tried reported that the device increased their ability to turn their heads because they no longer had to train their vision on a fixed point on the horizon, apparently something agoraphobics have to do in order to navigate outside the home. All was not easy for Dr. Meldman; some patients at first were reluctant to wear the device because of its peculiar appearance, but eventually they relented. But even this embarrassment had good results: The teasing they received actually relaxed them! And Meldman's and thirty thousand other psychiatrists' spouses in America can now be silenced about their annoyance with the messiness of pipe cleaners in ash trays, candy dishes, and other bric-a-brac around the house.

Every third-year medical student learns Sir William Osler's aphorism: "If many drugs are used for a disease, all are insufficient." For agoraphobia, the following therapies have been offered either as cures or as effecting marked alleviation of the entity and/or its symptoms: self-desensitization, imipramine, tricyclic antidepressants and monoamine oxidase inhibitors, phenelzine, methohexitone assisted desensitization, colored tablets, modified flooding technique with propanolo, running, thiopentone sleep treatment, psychotherapy plus MAO inhibitor nortriptyline, family therapy, uncovering therapy, lobotomy, antenna on eyeglasses, psychoanalysis, contextual analysis therapy, paradoxical intention, subliminal exposure to cinè film, eidetic imagery, social reinforcement, implosion and flooding, prolonged exposure, desensitization, apotrepic therapy, flooding in vivo, group flooding, desensitization, systematic desensitization, reciprocal inhibition therapy, imaginal flooding, psychotherapy with a combined behavioral and dynamic approach.

Everything from lobotomy to contextual analysis, most of them alive and working well in the hands of their inventors or promoters. They are all innocent enough, except those that cut brain tissue and those that drug, leaving irreversible effects. However, they are not so innocent in terms of human values. Most of them—behavior modifications, desensitization, and the like—treat symptoms without looking at the meaning of the behavior. Emotions and behavior are played with as one would a toy or a pet. We search in vain for references to the social reality of the human beings in question, the ambitions, aspirations, or unique problems in their lives with which they may be grappling. This is not unique to behaviorists or to agoraphobics. All people with limited rhetorical capacity, those who have to use a variety of subterfuges to make their point, are similarly subjected to the panoply of humiliating and degrading clinical and therapeutic interventions. One characteristic emerges almost without exception: The patient is seen as simple-minded; his or her human rights are abused; the route to the cure is secondary to the cure itself; the model is medical or "imitation medical," as if one were dealing with a comatose patient and administering medication to bring him around.

Psychoanalysis and the psychotherapies are exceptions; at least here the patients' "problems" are listened to. But the clinicians consider this form of therapy to be needlessly time-consuming and least effective. However misguided in substance the psychotherapies may be, at least they are rational, devoid of gimmickry, and do not treat grown adults as simple-minded, uncensorious cripples. None, including psychoanalysis, even entertains the possibility that the agoraphobic is engaged in an activity for her own purpose that will be changed or modified only in accordance with changing circumstances and times.

For those people with metaphorical diseases we may take a liberty with Osler's quotation: "If many drugs are used for a disease, there may be no disease." We are now in a clinical era of history where untoward human actions and behavior are most comfortably thought of as diseases, a reaction perhaps to the former religious belief that strange actions were due to evil spirits or being possessed. "Diseased" sounds more scientific and has greater appeal to the modern mind. No longer are people to be exorcised; they are to be treated. This new shift led George Bernard Shaw to remark that the world may soon become one gigantic hospital. Here the new classes would be for "doctors" and "patients," reversing roles periodically of course to relieve the boredom, as children do when playing cowboys and Indians.

14

A Modicum of Respect, Please

There are many therapists actively engaged in curing agoraphobics. Patients as well as doctors report cures, or at least miraculous changes, after only twenty sessions, sometimes even after twenty minutes. There are reports of sufferers who had been unable to leave the house for seven to ten years, who after a few sessions with this or that therapist are now able to go to the supermarket or shopping center completely unattended. In most instances the therapy is of the supportive or reassurance variety where the therapist (usually male) reassures the trembling, timid patient (usually female) that everything will be all right. And sure enough, there she is driving her car to the store. This usually occurs after five years of psychoanalysis, which did no good.

Of course psychoanalysis didn't work, nor should it. Rarely is the treatment nonsexist. Women should not respond to pejorative goals and expectations, giving a high-status, intellectual male psychoanalyst the pride of a cure. And in any case, it is wrong to speak of "curing" agoraphobics. The phobic patient is a living caricature of what she is living through. She has it within her power to relinquish the symptom whenever she feels it is the proper time and place.

There is some solace, gratification, satisfaction, and even revenge, however, in attributing the cure to a lesser-status, ingenuous male. Then seeing how important she can be, she suddenly cures him of his sense of inferiority and insignificance. In agoraphobia the client cures the therapist. The therapist then often includes her in the therapy team at his clinic where she can now claim professional status. The therapist, having the degree and the access to medical journals and media, reports the cure that he has effected. The cure comes from a male, but the kind of person with whom the patient, in her enforced status of inferiority, can identify.

She is not about to feed the already inflated vanity of an exalted psychoanalyst, a person whose elevated status is similar to that of her husband, who is paying the bills. She therefore bestows her gift of cure on the lowly and needy, rather than on the already bloated in whose shadow she has been forced to live: first with father, then with husband. She has gone beyond the awe, reverence, and deference that she was trained to feel toward male authority and dominance. Psychoanalysis has described the phenomenon of the analysand's not improving after "complete" insight, calling it "negative therapeutic response"—the analysand's resisting the giving up of symptoms—but psychoanalysis has not understood the importance of status and power as core elements in this drama.

Jean Baker Miller discusses the negative therapeutic response as it pertains to women analysands in general.* This is a most reasonable response for women. Having been taught the goals and blessings of autonomy, as a result of the analysis they find that this ideal state of being has little relevance for them. In the real world, because of lack of opportunity and personal resources, as well as material and acquired skills, autonomy is not only impossible, its attainment might be downright dangerous. It would undo the security and vicarious gratifications that do exist, due largely to a woman's adaptation as dependent and largely non- or quasiautonomous.

Miller's critique would have more validity if the real goal for women in analytic therapy were autonomy. It is excep-

---

* *Toward a New Psychology of Women* (Boston: Beacon Press, 1976), p. 93.

tional to find an analyst who sees the woman's cure coming through standing on her own two feet. The analytic goal for the woman has always been to abjure, renounce, or purge herself of those distractions, usually in public places, which might interfere with her biological role.

If the purpose of life is to nurture, this in turn demands dependence, submissiveness, and passivity. Therefore, the woman's negative therapeutic response may in fact be a genuine, self-protective defense against conventional stereotypic presumptions, rather than a frustration about being unable to actualize the autonomy being held out to her.

It may be doing a disservice to women to discard autonomy for them simply because it has served men well, although one can argue against the reflex imitation of male attributes. Can we then hope that women will have the opportunity to achieve those qualities that go hand-in-hand with full development of personage? Autonomy might fall into this category, attractively neuter.

What a sad state of affairs if women seeking liberation labeled those things unfairly withheld from them or attainable only with great difficulty as masculine and therefore undesirable. They would set up a separation and segregation as bad as that which has been imposed on them and only perpetuate the double-standard mental health concept. Jean Baker Miller gives us an important overall warning. In the new liberation women must take care to become creative and innovative, not imitative.

It is appropriate at this point to discuss individual human rights as they pertain to interpersonal relationships in general and to therapy relationships in particular.

Children growing up in environments of repression, inequity, and social deprivation, either by parental design or group custom, may often suffer irreparable harm, just as they would from lack of love or attention. We are referring to an upbringing marked by chronic invasions of privacy, violation of confidences, suppression of divergent views, limitations on freedom of association, movement, and making of outside contacts on the one hand, and the imposition through coercion of a panoply of mystical, religious, or irrational beliefs on the other. The latter are usually manifested as told to the child to augment parental control and power. These misrepresentations take place before the child has the cognitive ability to make choices or critical judgments. The family stories and legends abound with imagery that promotes magical beliefs, contains hidden threats, and generally makes a mockery of science and knowledge. Added to this is the imposition of various sexual and gender stereotypes that lead to inequities in personal growth and fulfillment. Children have routinely been coerced and misinformed, deceived and fooled about what they are and what they might become by parents who sincerely believe themselves to be helpful. We have only recently discovered how destructive these deceptions àre to both sexes, but especially to girls. Daughters have universally grown up believing in their own inferiority. We—and they— have accepted this state of affairs.

These falsehoods and injustices may cause more difficulties for the emerging individual than all the errant libidinal and aggressive demiurges combined. The "therapeutic" process, designed and offered to correct the mistakes of the past, should be expected to show a special sensitivity to the issues of human rights (justice, fair play, equality). Minimally, we expect therapy not to repeat these past errors.

Therapists often ride roughshod over our higher ideals of human rights and respect for the individual. The cure repeats the disease, this time by other "helpers" who are supposed to have the best of curative intentions, high motives, and ethical principles. Yet therapists make light of such matters as privacy and confidentiality for the benefits derived from group or third-party exposures: they unselfconsciously record or videotape sessions; they drug patients into conforming to desired behavior with powerful chemicals that can cure nothing, but may cause habituation and addiction as well as a host of untoward and at times irreversible side effects.

Fooling the patient into health is the prevailing model for cure today. The paradoxical pride of behaviorists and biochemists in getting rid of the symptoms but leaving the cause epitomizes this stance. Is this different from the magic fairy tales of childhood? It is especially ironic that this mode of treatment is not formed in any other branch of science, physical or social. What physician treats only the cough or the jaundiced skin? What firefighter rushes to destroy the alarm system or smoke detector?

In the same vein, the use of placebo is growing as accepted and recommended practice. It is used therapeutically in individual instances as well as a research tool. In the latter, there is some justification if the people are fully informed about and fully understand its possible use. However, to treat with a placebo without revealing its nature is a deception and a manipulation that surely undoes any salutary result that might accrue.

We insist that the structure of therapy and the rules governing the behavior of therapist and client are of central importance. The manner in which therapist and client conduct themselves is crucial if we are to undo past atrocities; it also affects how we behave in our other relationships. A therapeutic relationship in which human rights are scrupulously honored will always be ultimately more successful than all the miraculous cures achieved through coercion, mystification, or deception. Nowhere is respect for the dignity of the individual more flagrantly violated than in the myriad of treatments devised to cure phobias.

15

Beyond Clinical Diagnosis

WOMEN ARE OUR POOR

The very poor and the very wealthy frequently cannot leave their homes for money reasons. The former often do not have bus or subway fare, and walking does not get one very far. Furthermore, there are too many temptations in every store and window; having thrust in one's face the things that are for others but not for oneself or one's family is too much. What if one should get hungry? Most restaurants are off limits financially. The problem is compounded if children are along: It is humiliating not to be able to buy a child a candy bar when he sees other children have them in abundance.

It is against the law in most states to be found without money in one's pocket; one can be arrested for vagrancy. It is a fact of life that poor people, those who are shabbily dressed, and members of minorities are routinely excluded from certain areas of the city. Poor women run the risk of questioning by police and being included in roundups of prostitutes. Although it is the affluent who have made the most noise about their own safety, the streets have never been safe for the poor.

People on limited and fixed incomes have become housebound because of galloping inflation. What was an adequate retirement income several years ago is no longer enough. The elderly find themselves literally priced out of the *agora*.

Leaving the home for them becomes nightmarish. The fear of being assaulted is verbalized in terms of criminals on the street but it must also encompass the alienation that comes with being reduced to second-class citizenship economically. So although purist clinicians might object, we are justified in talking about "economic agoraphobia," a marketplace now strange and unfriendly, out of reach and at the same time agonizingly tempting.

Another deterrent to leaving home or one's neighborhood is what has been labeled "functional illiteracy," the inability to read want ads, bus and street signs, menus, and so on. It is now estimated that 22 percent of our white population and as many as 44 percent of our nonwhite population are functionally illiterate. For them, the outer world has so many dangers that the peasant's life, living and dying within five miles of their home, becomes their social and psychological reality. These are the "silent" handicapped. More than functional illiterates, they become functional agoraphobics. Straying beyond what they are used to can result in anxieties and even panic. Yet they are not and probably should not be classified as clinical problems. They are the forgotten people who are dependent on others to traverse areas beyond walking distance.

EVEN THOSE WHO LEAD ARE OFTEN PLAGUED

Agoraphobia may indeed be the hidden disease, affecting many of our female leaders at some time in their lives. Charlotte Perkins Gilman had it—until she left her husband. Jane Addams became depressed when she was twenty-one years old. She was wealthy, well educated, and wanted to study medicine. She fell into a "nervous depression" that paralyzed her for seven years. She was gripped by a "sense of futility, of misdirected energy. It was doubtless true that I was weary of myself and sick of asking what I am and what I ought to be."*

* Barbara Ehrenreich and Dierdre English, *"For Her Own Good": 150 Years of the Experts' Advice to Women* (Garden City, N.Y.: Anchor Press, 1979), p. 2.

Margaret Sanger was another case. She was twenty years old and apparently happily married. She had had tuberculosis, but was making a good recovery. Suddenly she became bed-ridden. When relatives asked her what she wanted to do, she replied, "Nothing." When they asked her where she wanted to go, she replied, "Nowhere."

This was during a period when no diagnosis would have been made about female ennui, which included dissatisfaction with life intellectually or socially. An obstetrics textbook of the period, for example, declared that woman "has a head almost too small for intellect but just big enough for love."*

Charlotte Perkins Gilman, in keeping a journal of her illness—her inability to get out of bed, her extreme fatigue upon performing simple household chores—noted that her sickness vanished when she was away from her home, her husband, and her child, and returned as soon as she came back to them. Her doctor, S. Weir Mitchell of rest-cure fame, dismissed her journal as evidence of self-conceit. Gilman describes his prescription for her: "Live as domestic a life as possible. Have your child with you all the time. (Be it remarked that if I did but dress the baby it left me shaking and crying—certainly far from a healthy companionship for her, to say nothing of the effect on me.) Lie down an hour after each meal. Have but two hours intellectual life a day. And never touch pen, brush or pencil as long as you live."**

A contrast to the rebels is Sara Teasdale who, although never considered a major poet, won the Pulitzer Prize and saw her books on the bestseller list.

Teasdale suffered from chronic "low vitality" and an overwhelming need to be, or to appear to be, complaisant and feminine. "I don't want to be a 'literary woman.' Art can never mean to a woman what it does mean to a man. Love means

* Quoted in Richard H. Shryock, ed., *Medicine in America; Historical Essays* (Baltimore: Johns Hopkins Press, 1966), p. 184.
** *The Living of Charlotte Perkins Gilman: An Autobiography* (New York: Harper Colophon Books, 1975), p. 96.

that," she wrote.* For her, love meant worshipping a sublime and powerful man.

When she was thirty she married Ernst Filsinger, a St. Louis businessman. She abhorred direct self-assertion (she hated feminists) and she resorted to every manner of covert activity to keep herself sane, that is, to have time to write. Despite her statements that motherhood was woman's noblest calling, her only pregnancy was terminated by abortion. Her low vitality prevented her from traveling with her husband on his business trips. His return was usually followed by her own immediate departure to the country for a rest cure. In the country she would write. During one eighteen-month period she and Ernst lived together for a total of six weeks. She killed herself at age forty-eight.

Katha Pollit writes: "[For Teasdale], the price of ambition was not spinsterhood but redoubled efforts to prove her femininity through marriage and to disclaim competition with men by keeping her work small and delicate and pleasant. . . . If it is in the lives of Brontë, Dickinson, Rossetti, and Barrett that we see the price they paid for their gifts, it is in the poems of Teasdale that we feel the price she paid for hers."**

The present-day emphasis on the family as "the means for saving Western civilization" is not new. The 1909 White House Conference on the Care of Dependent Children declared that "home life is the highest and finest product of civilization."

Despite such pronouncements, nineteenth-century Americans showed little interest in home as a physical place. During the 1820s, entire communities packed up and went west. The home, where mother sat ready to tend our every need, was often forgotten as children went off on their own—sons to find their fortunes, daughters with their husbands. The idea of home became predominant after World War II when the

* *The New York Times Book Review*, December 23, 1979.
** Ibid.

American dream became a ranch house in the suburbs with plenty of grass for children to play on.

One sidelight of the postwar emphasis on home and motherhood was the promise of what such an absorption held for the mediocre: "You do not have to be clever, and you do not even have to think if you do not want to. You may have been hopeless at arithmetic at school; or perhaps all your friends got scholarships but you couldn't stand the sight of a history book and so failed and left school early; or perhaps you would have done well if you hadn't had measles just before the exam. Or you may be really clever. But all this does not matter, and it hasn't anything to do with whether or not you are a good mother. If a child can play with a doll, you can be an ordinary devoted mother."*

Women's total immersion in the home was futher prescribed by popularization of the concept that children need mothering (no substitute would do) twenty-four hours a day, seven days a week. Anything less would harm the child for life. John Bowlby wrote: "Just as the baby needs to feel that he belongs to his mother, the mother needs to feel that she belongs to her child and it is only when she has the satisfaction of this feeling that it is easy for her to devote herself to him. The provision of constant attention day and night, seven days a week and 365 in the year, is possible only for a woman who derives profound satisfaction from seeing her child grow from babyhood, through the many phases of childhood to become an independent man or woman, and knows that it is her care which has made this possible."**

Living in this kind of imposed separate world—the world of women and children—would obviously create a separatist culture for women. The culture would as a matter of course create personalities who were alienated from the mainstream society. Jessie Bernard writes "a word about a kind of patho-

---

* D. W. Winnicott, *Mother and Child: A Primer of First Relationships* (New York: Basic Books, 1957), p. vii.

** *Maternal Care and Mental Health* (New York: Schocken Books, 1966), p. 67.

logical separatism. Not because it is propounded by anyone as a model but only because it exists as a reality for many women, the passive retreatist separation of despair is accorded a bow here. During the Hitler era there were individuals who could neither leave the country nor yet stomach what was going on around them. They huddled together in what they called 'internal migration.' They left the scene mentally, dropped out emotionally, and withdrew into their own sheltered world. In their work lives they might 'collaborate' in the sense that they did not actively fight the system. But in their personal lives they were separatists. Citizens in occupied countries may also engage in this kind of separatism. In public they may accept the enemy's assimilative co-optation; in private they remain separatist, uninvolved, even alienated. The research on female depression is illuminating here."*

The retreatist separation of despair is the mode of the agoraphobic. She refuses to collaborate in any aspect of life.

* "Homosociality of Female Depression," *Journal of Social Issues,* 32 (1976): 207–24.

16

Under House Arrest: Legally
Induced Agoraphobia

Robert and Florence Krellman didn't want to pay $10,268 the IRS said they owed. Robert said their petition to the Tax Court was mailed on the last day of the court's filing deadline. But postal equipment put three postmarks on the envelope—all of them illegible. So, the Krellmans had it typed and gave it to an employee to mail that day.

The employee recalls mailing it then or the next day; he wasn't sure which. There's a big hole in this story, the IRS asserted: Robert didn't explain how he got Florence to come from their Great Neck, N.Y. home to his Manhattan office to sign the petition. More likely: He took it home, she signed it and he had it mailed the next day, a day late, the IRS said. It needn't have happened that way, the court concluded.

"We can think of many possible scenarios other than that of Florence chained to her kitchen stove in [their] home on Long Island," the court asserted, and determined the petition was mailed in time.

Wall Street Journal, September 26, 1979

The structure and content of common law has kept women in the home, has punished women for being elsewhere, and has been, in a very real sense, agoraphobic in its approach to female citizens.

A well-known common law provision, changing slowly, is that a woman's "domicile," if she is married, is that of her husband. If, for example, a woman gets a job in a state other than where she has lived with her husband and moves there to work, she has been, until recently guilty of desertion. On the other hand, if a husband gets a job in another state, notifies his wife (even by wire) that he (they) have moved there, and she does not follow, she is also guilty of desertion.

Married women who have failed to follow their husbands to new domiciles have been denied their rights to vote, have been asked to leave state colleges where they were matriculated as state residents, and have been forced to pay income tax in a state where the husband, but not the wife, lived and worked. In *Green v. Commissioner of Corporations and Taxation* (364 Mass. 389, 1973), the Supreme Judicial Court of Massachusetts held that income received by Mrs. Green while she lived in New Hampshire was subject to Massachusetts tax by virtue of the established common law rule "that a wife's domicile, absent some marital wrong committed by her husband, follows that of her husband." Since similar taxes are not levied on a husband, we can correctly deduce agoraphobia by the courts only when they are considering women, whose place is in the home of the husband's choosing.

A wife was forced to file for divorce in a state where she does not live, and not in her own state of residence, because the former is where her husband lives (*Meeker v. Meeker*, 52 N.J. 59, 1968). In this case the Supreme Court of New Jersey held that the Meekers could not file for divorce in New Jersey, although both desired to do so, because while the wife lived there (both had at the time of their marriage), the husband now lived in Pennsylvania.

These decisions on domicile reflect a centuries-old tradition that determines not only the legal, but the equally critical social and economic conditions of marriage for women. Women were generally considered the property of their husbands, and of course, one can move property at will.

A seventeenth-century description of the perfect wife: "when shee submits herselfe with quietness, cheerefully, even as a well-broken horse turns at the least check of the riders bride, readily going and standing as he wishes that sits upon his back."* In early common law the metaphor of horse-breaking is used frequently to describe training one's wife.

* William Whatley, "A Bride-Bush or a Wedding Sermon," quoted in Kathleen Davies, "'The Sacred Condition of Equality'—how original were

During the nineteenth century many communities were formed on both sides of the Atlantic Ocean to explore socialist and communal ways of living. The concepts of division of labor and ownership were challenged, revised, and changed. One concept of division of labor remained the same: The woman's place was in the home; women were responsible for household chores and for children.

Plans for the collectivization of housework were devised, but the plans all assumed that the women of the community (collectively, rather than individually) would do the domestic labor. According to Barbara Taylor, "Occasionally a real iconoclast would attack the sexual division of labor itself; interestingly, however, it was usually children who were suggested as appropriate substitutes for mundane household tasks. . . . At no point was male responsibility for childcare proposed."*

This reaction of "radicals" to the housework situation was paralleled in the 1960s when the New Left women finally rose in protest against their men and founded the radical wing of the women's liberation movement. They protested that although they had given up the bourgeois notions of marriage, of husbands supporting wives, and of suburban dwelling units, they, the women, were still responsible for the housecleaning, for the cooking and shopping, and for the childcare.

Their mothers had cooked the steak and potatoes; they were cooking the brown rice. Division of labor had not changed at all, and these women were perhaps even less secure than their mothers had been, since their fathers had at least paid lip service to the concept that men should take care of their women.

After initially favoring the idea of female equality, revolutionary governments in France became increasingly hostile to women in politics. In 1793 women's clubs were disbanded; in 1795 women were barred from participating in any political

---

Puritan doctrines of marriage?" *Social History*, 5 (May 1977): 572.

* "The men are as bad as their masters . . . : Socialism, Feminism, and Sexual Antagonism in the London Tailoring Trade in the Early 1830's," *Feminist Studies*, 5, 1 (Spring 1979).

event. In 1793 the *Journal des révolutions de Paris* spelled out the only acceptable role for the "bonne citoyenne": "Citizenesses, be honest and hardworking daughters, chaste and tender wives, and wise mothers and you will be good patriots. True patriotism consists in fulfilling your duties . . . not in wearing the bonnet, trousers, pistols and pike. Leave that to men, born to protect you and make you happy." Women who stepped beyond these boundaries were accused of "anti-civic and perfidious intentions."* The Napoleonic Code catalogued such ideas, placing women under the jurisdiction of father or husband.

A similar reversion occurred following the Cuban revolution in the 1960s. During the fighting, women and men fought side-by-side to build the new order. Shortly thereafter, more traditional patterns reasserted themselves, and the women were told, "Now that we have won our revolution you may return to the home."

No matter what century we examine, no matter what country, the woman's place is in the home.

The United States Supreme Court spoke to this issue, and resolved it in an unambiguous manner. The Court said, in *Hoyt v. Florida* (368 U.S. 57) (1961): "Despite the enlightened emancipation of women from the restrictions and protections of bygone years, and their entry into many parts of community life formerly considered to be reserved to men, woman is still regarded as the center of home and family life. We cannot say that it is constitutionally impermissible for a State, acting in pursuit of the general welfare, to conclude that a woman should be relieved from the civil duty of jury service unless she herself determines that such service is consistent with her own special responsibilities." This was the law of the land until very recently.

If the duties of a citizen are considered secondary for a woman to those centering in her home, it should not be surprising that citizenship itself is not the right of married fe-

* Cited in Gerard Walker, *La Révolution française vue par ses journeaux* (Paris: Tardy, 1948), pp. 409–10.

males acting on their own. As domicile follows husband, so does citizenship.

The Supreme Court upheld a statute that provided that although an American male did not suffer loss of citizenship during his marriage to a foreign citizen, an American woman did (*Schneider* v. *Rusk*, 377 U.S. 162) (1964).

Under Henry VIII, who is remembered for, among other things, how he treated women who were married to him, the law was written that "married women, along with infants, idiots, and those of non sane memory" were unable to make wills. Apparently marriage caused a loss of understanding and volition. Most states, including New York, have had similar statutes. When a woman married, any previous will she might have made was automatically annulled. In a marriage, under French law, a sane wife is not even the legal equal of a mad husband.

The medical profession went hand-in-hand with the legal profession in including women with incompetents. For example, in an article on the causes of melancholia written in 1857, women and men are considered to be in separate categories for the purpose of treatment and diagnosis. "The moral affections are the most frequent cause of melancholia. Disappointed affection, jealousy, fear, which is the perception of a future ill, or one which threatens us; and fright, which is the perception of a present ill, are the passions, which produce the greatest number of melancholiacs, particularly in youth, among women, and in the lowest classes of society: whilst ambition, avarice, wounded self-love, reverses of fortune and gaming, are the most frequent causes of insanity among adults and men of mature age, in the higher classes of society, and in those countries whose customs and institutions foster all the social passions."*

We see once again that a troubled woman is supposed to have had disappointment in her emotional life, and that a trou-

---

* Dr. Daniel H. Tuke, London, England, *The Asylum Journal of Mental Science*, published by authority of The Association of Medical Officers of Asylums and Hospitals for the Insane, vol. III, no. 21 (1857), pp. 239–40.

bled man is assumed to have suffered a setback with his fortunes in the outer world. If a woman was deprived of the control of even her own property, it is easy to see why her existence was forced to be bound by her emotions—they were all she was left with, particularly after marriage.

The concept of the *foyer* (home, hearth) and of women's place in it is clearly expressed in an aspect of French marriage law that provided that adultery by husbands was punishable only by light sanctions, unless the offense was actually committed in his home, in which case it was cause for divorce. Adultery by wives anywhere was cause for divorce and sometimes imprisonment. In France women did not receive the right to vote until 1945 (their participation in the Resistance was frequently cited as justification for giving them the vote).

Under present Greek law, the man is head of the household and makes all decisions concerning his wife and family. He can, for example, refuse to let his wife work outside the home. If he makes an important decision without consulting his wife, she can take him to court for abusing his authority. But so long as he asks her, he does not have to take any notice of her objections because legally he has the last word.

In the 1830s, writers of advice for women, instead of bemoaning the legal inferiority of all women and particularly wives, encouraged them to submit to their husbands: "It is no derogation from the dignity or utility of woman to declare that she is inferior to man in moral as well as physical strength. She has a different part to act and therefore requires different qualities from the being who has been pronounced her superior by the Almighty himself. Woman was created avowedly to be the helpmeet, not the ruler, nor yet the equal of man. . . . A condition, just subordinant to that of man, is replete with usefulness and consistency."*

The Almighty was also called upon in the state of Illinois

* From Virginia Cary, *Letters on Female Character, Addressed to a Young Lady on the Death of Her Mother,* 2d ed., enlarged (Richmond, Va., 1830), pp. 21–22.

in 1872 to assure women and men that it was God's will that women not be allowed to practice law.

> It is also to be remembered that women attorneys at law were unknown in England, and a proposition that a woman should enter the courts of Westminster Hall in that capacity, or as a barrister, would have created hardly less astonishment than one that she should ascend the bench of bishops, or be elected to a seat in the House of Commons.
>
> . . . That God designed the sexes to occupy different spheres of action, and that it belonged to men to make, apply, and execute the laws, was regarded as an almost axiomatic truth. In view of these facts, we are certainly warranted in saying that when the legislature gave to this court the power of granting licenses to practice law, it was not with the slightest expectation that this privilege would be extended to women.*

A clear message is given to women of all social and economic classes: It is not safe to leave the home. Equally succinct is the message that it is dangerous to live alone. Women are taught to believe that it is safer to be with a man (who will protect) both outside and at home.

Overlooked is that many men are frail, old, unathletic, or weak. Such men are not given the same kind of advice, although it would be equally practical. Obviously some women are better able to defend themselves than some men.

Females living alone are told to list their numbers in the telephone book, and their names on apartment house directories, with only an initial. (Surely this tells all potential burglars or attackers that a woman lives there alone.)

Women are warned that "rape prevention at home is the one place you have the greatest control over your personal safety." The police write: "You should always give the impression that you do not live alone. If there is a person at your door, give them the impression that someone, preferably a man, is living with you. When the door bell rings, call out 'it's

---

* *Bradwell* v. *The State*, 83 U.S. 130 (December 1872).

all right Mike . . . I'll get it'. That alone will normally discourage any man that may have the wrong intentions."*

Of course we all want to discourage rapists and muggers.
But warnings such as these serve to keep women inside the
house, living with pretend Mikes. The police department also
advises women: "Never walk anywhere alone at night." Since
it gets dark about 4 P.M. during part of the winter, this advice is
practically a prescription for agoraphobia.

Law enforcement agencies and courts have traditionally
considered women more in need of protection, and have
deemed them coming of age at a later time, despite the fact
that girls mature physically sooner than boys. Until 1972 New
York State defined "persons in need of supervision" (PINS) as
"a male less than 16 years of age and a female less than 18
years of age who does not attend school . . . or who is incor-
rigible, ungovernable, or habitually disobedient and beyond
the lawful control of parents or other lawful authority."**

In *Matter of Patricia A.*, that part of the statute that covered
women between the ages of 16 and 18 was declared unconstitutional. The court said:

> The argument that discrimination against females on the
> basis of age is justified because of the obvious danger of preg-
> nancy in an immature girl and because of out-of-wedlock
> births which add to . . . welfare relief burdens . . . is with-
> out merit. It is enough to say that the contention completely
> ignores the fact that the statute covers far more than acts of
> sexual misconduct. But, beyond that, even if we were to as-
> sume that the legislation had been prompted by such consid-
> erations, there would have been no rational basis for exempt-
> ing from the PINS definition, the 16- and 17-year-old boy
> responsible for the girl's pregnancy or out-of-wedlock birth.
> As it is the conclusion seems inescapable that lurking behind
> the discrimination is the imputation that females who engage
> in misconduct, sexual or otherwise, ought more to be cen-

---

* Police Department, Crime Prevention Division, Syracuse, New York.
** New York Judiciary Law, Family Court Act 712(b) (McKinney Supp.
1971), p. 38.

sured, and their conduct subject to greater control and regulation, than males.

[A] girl of 16 or 17 may not be subject to a possible loss of liberty for conduct which would be entirely licit for 16- or 17-year-old boys.*

Longer prison terms for women than for men convicted of the same crime have been declared unconstitutional under the Fourteenth Amendment. However, both longer and indeterminate terms for women (which resulted in their serving longer periods of time) have been the practice in most of our judicial systems. The rationale for such differentiation of treatment was summarized by a New Jersey judge in September 1972. Frederick W. Hall stated it could be argued that women should be treated differently from men, because they "were more amenable and responsive to rehabilitation and reform which might, however, require a longer period of confinement."

Does society feel obligated to punish women offenders more harshly because they have broken the taboo of leaving the home in the first place, "going public" in crime?

Until recently in this country, there were separate airplane flights available for men (message: Women don't really belong on airplanes). Although many states have declared that sex segregation and discrimination in public accommodations are illegal, the U.S. Supreme Court has held that a restaurant can segregate facilities on the basis of sex, the state act of licensing the establishment not being sufficient in the eyes of the court to constitute state action.

Private clubs that discriminate on the basis of sex are still legal, although many persons consider them objectionable, including the U.S. Department of Justice, which requested during Carter's presidency that judges who sit on the federal bench resign (if temporarily) from them.

These clubs, like those of London and the cafes in southern Europe, inform women that they are not welcome in the

---

* 31 N.Y. 2d, at 88–89; 335 N.Y.S. 2d, at 37–38.

marketplace. Taken alone, this deprivation would not be crushing, but combined with so many other such exclusionary messages, the inexorable cumulative effects take their toll despite a few late-coming remedies. Besides the moral hurt here, women doing business are placed at a distinct disadvantage.

In 1908, the Supreme Court decided the case of *Muller* v. *Oregon,* which dealt with the issue of so-called protective legislation for women workers. Many enlightened people of that time, including Samuel Gompers, argued that protective legislation should extend to *all* workers. The Court, in its decision, incorporated the current sociological thinking on woman's proper sphere into the definitive law of the land.

> That woman's physical structure and the performance of maternal functions place her at a disadvantage in the struggle for subsistence is obvious. This is especially true when the burdens of motherhood are upon her . . . as healthy mothers are essential to vigorous offspring, the physical well-being of woman becomes an object of public interest and care in order to preserve the strength and vigor of the race.
>
> . . . The two sexes differ in structure of body, and in the functions to be performed by each.*

The same rationale that kept women out of higher education was being used to keep them out of gainful, equal employment. It was used to justify special legislation for women and to uphold their exclusion from specific occupations, such as bartending and mining; job classifications, such as restricting those that require weight lifting beyond a certain limit, or overtime work; periods of employment, such as the regulation of women's work before and after childbirth; and from compulsory jury duty.

A lawyer and businesswoman from Colombia tells us why the laws must be changed in her country, why at present it is extremely difficult for a woman to be anything but a housewife. She says she earns a higher salary than any woman in

* *Muller* v. *Oregon,* 208 U.S. 412 (1908).

Colombia, but for the past twenty years she has been trying to get a bank loan in her own name—with no success.

In Spain there are so few jobs for women that most females are dependent first on their fathers, and then on their husbands or the church; even if they can withstand the social disapproval of living on their own, they cannot afford it. Married women cannot dispose of property, apply for a passport, or even open a bank account without the approval of their husbands. Until 1972 a woman in Spain could not leave her parents' home before she was twenty-five without their permission, unless it was to get married or to enter a convent. (This has been reduced to age twenty-one.) At home, there is total isolation from public life.

It was not until 1894 that German universities granted women admission as matriculating students. Until 1908 women were prohibited from belonging to political organizations, and even barred from attending political meetings. Legally subject to her father until marriage, after marriage the German woman stood under the legal guardianship of her husband. She was required to get his permission in order to work outside the home, and she had to turn over to him the use of all property she brought into the marriage as well as the right of administration for all income jointly produced during the marriage.

The legal tradition in the United States is not very different. The tone was set by Blackstone in his commentaries on the common law: The husband and wife have one legal identity, that of the husband.

> By marriage, the husband and wife are one person in law.
> . . . The very being or legal existence of the woman is suspended during the marriage, or at least is incorporated and consolidated into that of the husband, under whose wing, protection, and cover she performs everything.

A married woman lost control not only of her real property (her land), but of her personal property. (Today, in some states the husband even owns his wife's clothing.) She could not make a contract in her own name, nor could she sue or be sued in her own name. The difficulty posed for women trying to get credit in their own names, even with the Equal Credit Opportunity Act, stems from this legacy of the English common law that makes married women nonpersons in the eyes of creditors.

If she worked outside the home, the husband was entitled to her wages. She even lacked the capacity for criminal responsibility: Crimes done by a woman in her husband's presence were assumed to be committed under his command, and he was held responsible for them.

Legal tradition has dictated that a woman's place is in the home, but ironically it has never been *her* home.

Hoyt was overruled in 1975 by *Taylor* v. *Louisiana,* when the Supreme Court held that the systematic exemption of women from juries constituted a violation of a rape defendant's 6th Amendment right to a jury representative of the community. (*Duren* v. *Mississippi,* in 1979, gave a further extension to equality between the sexes on juries when it overruled the option for women to decline jury duty when no such option was available to men.)

If as recently as 1961 women were excluded from juries, and as recently as 1979 women had exemptions available to them that men could not use, then there is clear evidence that the burdens and benefits of citizenship have not been equal between the sexes in modern times.

If a New York State judge could say in 1970, "Her lament should be addressed to the Nineteenth Amendment State of Womanhood which prefers cleaning and cooking, rearing of children and television soap operas, bridge and canasta, the beauty parlor and shopping, to becoming embroiled in plaintiff's problems,"* we know that women have not been welcome in the *agora.*

---

* *DeKosenko* v. *Brandt,* 63 Misc. 2d 895, 313 N.Y.S. 2d 830 (Sup. Ct. 1970).

17

Male Agoraphobia: Macho and Market

In his new Jerusalem a person who dislikes work will be
sorry he was born.

"Vespers"
W. H. Auden

Throughout this book we have focused exclusively on female agoraphobia, since it is overwhelmingly a female strata-
gem. But a society that punishes women by definition also
punishes men. Thus it is important to look at men who are
unable to conform to their "role" in the male marketplace.

Freud realized that street fear in men was a metaphor for
not wanting to go to work. It had little to do with streets,
bridges, elevators, and the like, as the modern-day behaviorists believe, befuddling their clients. With rare exception, unless he is extremely wealthy or part of the counterculture, it is
not acceptable for the male openly to abjure work. If for reasons of his own, working in our world is not to his liking, he
must devise ways of getting out of it while at the same time
reciting the litany of the male work ethic.

A male's desire not to work has to be repressed as the
female's drive to do so must often be. The taboo for the male
may be stronger than it is for the woman. A few men, principally of the counterculture, have been able to verbalize such
feelings, but even then it is expressed as sitting it out (like
Achilles) until after the revolution, not wanting to contribute
to a corrupt society. These men do not assume the role of
passivity; instead they do their own thing—farming, crafts,

drugs. Most of them slowly drift back to the security of the macho pack.

Perhaps principally because they are afforded no alternative, men may be anxious about the burdens and glories of leadership and achievement; they may secretly harbor resentment about having to work, to provide, and to assume burdens that shorten their lives. Agoraphobia, chronic or episodic, may be the overt manifestation of their resentment, a bitterness that for the male has no acceptable outlet. It may be that most men have experienced episodic agoraphobia as unexplained momentary panic seemingly unconnected with palpable danger. Being in the great out-of-doors or in an area representing male achievement, dominance, and supremacy can cause fear and trembling.

Mainstream psychoanalysis took it for granted that in order to be a mature adult, a man worked and achieved, mated and fathered, dominated and taught; in these the male acted rather than being acted upon. In contrast to the female, whose main calamity in life was to lose love, disaster for the male meant to be defeated or otherwise to suffer diminution.

Boys have traditionally not competed with girls, so that they might never risk the possibility of being defeated by a female. Indeed, a major reason given to keep girls out of Little League was that if a nine-year-old boy struck out to a girl pitcher, he would be psychologically damaged for life. It was taken for granted as a natural prerogative that the male would and should prevail over the female without the slightest doubt or qualm.

Do men indeed feel guilty about their unwon and unearned advantages in life? Does it bother them that they invariably and inevitably are expected to eclipse their sisters in worldly matters?

The matter of male guilt has heretofore been considered largely a question of resolving Oedipal conflict, the young male's feeling of culpability for displacing the father. Psychoanalytic literature rarely mentions that a male might feel the slightest qualm about unfairly winning out over or defeating a mother, wife, daughter, or sister.

The new consciousness of the feminist movement can benefit the analysis of certain male patients who have not responded to past traditional interpretations that were simply wide of the mark. For example, men who have ambivalent feelings toward women, feelings that originated with their sisters, have been poorly understood. In the past they would have been interpreted in the light of incest compounded with sibling rivalry. Other dimensions of their relationships, such as worry about a sister's destiny, were rarely explored. Societal influences have frequently minimized a brother's feelings of guilt.

Yet many men do feel the consequences of their aggression over their sisters (if only in the form of succeeding, when the female cannot). Tennessee Williams addressed this problem in *The Glass Menagerie,* where he showed his sensitivity to the plight of a sister—through the agony of the brother. Tom Wingfield is troubled by his abandonment of his lame sister, Laura. At the close of the play he says:

> I traveled around a great deal. The cities swept about me like dead leaves, leaves that were brightly colored but torn away from the branches. I would have stopped, but I was pursued by something. It always came upon me unawares, taking me altogether by surprise. Perhaps it was only a piece of transparent glass.
>
> . . . Then all at once my sister touches my shoulder. I turn around and look into her eyes.
>
> . . . Oh, Laura, Laura, I tried to leave you behind me, but I am more faithful than I intended to be!

The price paid by the sister of a successful brother is palpable and poignant. The effects on the successful brother are far subtler, a chronic feeling of guilt derived from an unearned advantage and a victory over a sister who was foredoomed to anonymity the minute he was born. This is the stuff of which countless successful brothers are made: an agony of conscience that increased success only aggravates.

Most sisters dutifully submit to self-obliteration for the

conventional compensations that society has to offer them. Many will be wrecked by the injustices of this almost reflex oppression.

Freud called the male's guilt feelings part of the "fear of success" syndrome—an affliction of men who are undone by success and characteristically collapse at the pinnacle of their triumphs. However, these feelings always relate to one's father or brother, never to a sister.

Freud described episodes in his own life of acute anxiety or temporary disorientation that occurred in public places. One incident happened on his first visit to the Acropolis in Athens. He suffered what his brother, who accompanied him, described as "a peculiar disbelief in the reality of what was before his eyes."

Later, in a self-analysis of the phenomenon, Freud claimed that he could not believe that he, from his previous impoverished student days, would be in a position to visit such a wonderful place. He connected this with a forbidden wish to excel over his father. The conflict with father makes success, achieving the heights, a frightening area. Taking nothing away from the gravity of Freud's dilemma, we must admire his choice of location for its enactment. Where else would it be fitting for a giant to feel agoraphobic? Can we imagine panic gripping Freud in a supermarket or at Ebbet's Field?

Although the male's ability to work and to go far in the world was the keystone of mental health for Freud, he sensed that the achiever could be beset with problems. In a section entitled "Some Character-types Met with in Psychoanalytic Work," he told of "those wrecked by success." Here, because of a sense of guilt, people might become mentally ill when they achieved in reality those things they had savored in fantasy. Freud tells of a teacher who fell into a deep melancholia when he succeeded a master who had trained him. Here, Freud writes, "the forces of conscience which induce illness in consequence of success . . . are closely connected with the Oedipus Complex . . . as perhaps, indeed is our sense of guilt in general."

Freud's reductionism on this point is incorrect. There are a hundred valid reasons for melancholia, or for a person to retreat. Those whom the retreat inconveniences may choose not to see the reasons, but they exist nonetheless.

Children know little about the complex machinations and intrigues of the marketplace. They do become aware of open spaces, massive edifices, the movements of seeming armies of people, and the dangerous speed of vehicles. When observing people, children realize that those moving, working, and rushing are largely males, while women tend to remain at home. Children witness the tensions that develop between parents, noting the differences in behavior of the two sexes—division of labor, emotional reactions, leisuretime occupations, and sometimes attitudes toward lovemaking and even physical assaults. Yet in the evening the inside is warm and comfortable; the outside, dark, cold, and forbidding.

Moreover, the largely parent-serving fairy tales, bedtime stories, as well as religious training, tell of unseen monsters and spirits lurking in both the underworld and the open skies. In addition to the spirits, the child is routinely warned against the ubiquitous stranger outside the home who seduces, molests, abuses, and kidnaps.

From all this, and indeed from every aspect in a child's developmental environment, comes the matter of gender formation and stereotyping. The young boy is discouraged from participating in inside activity with the women; he is discouraged from playing with dolls, hanging around his mother or sister, or puttering in the kitchen lest he become feminine. Parents and teachers push children into their proper gender roles and all too often there is no room for tolerance of bisexual identification to gratify the passive or tender needs of a boy or the assertive, outgoing needs of a girl. The gender imperatives that parents rigidly impose on their childen almost from birth may be responsible for much of the infantile neurosis formerly attributed to psychosexual, i.e., Oedipal, conflicts.

The youngest agoraphobic described in literature was a

boy less than five years old.* His father, a Viennese physician, consulted Sigmund Freud in 1909 for the problem he was having with the child. Freud never dealt directly with the child, getting the information mainly from the father, a dubious practice at best. Yet from this protocol we gain information about a severe infantile neurosis where the principal symptom is the fear of going out in the street—classic agoraphobia.

This is the case of "Little Hans," who suddenly would not go out of doors. When questioned by his family, he said that he was afraid that a big and heavy horse would bite him or that a big and heavy horse might fall on him. His fear also extended to carts, furniture vans, and buses. No amount of reassurance could persuade him to venture outside the protection of his house.

The alleged significant event of his life was the birth of his sister when he was three and a half years old. Her presence apparently presented him with seemingly unresolvable problems with his parents, which led to the neurotic solution— displacing all pain outside the home. In addition, Hans changed the adversary from father to huge horse, which would destroy the diminutive son.

Freud explained this neurosis not on the basis that Hans was "a neurotic degenerate," as was the custom of the times, but rather that he was victim of the Oedipal Complex, the psychosexual theory that was to become the keystone of Freud's developmental scenario. Hans became acutely fearful of retribution (castration) from his father because of his sexual feelings toward his mother, now accentuated by competition with the new sister. His fear was heightened by the observation that some small children were somehow deprived of little "widdlers." (He feared that little children became castrated—

* Sigmund Freud, *Analysis of a Phobia in a Five-year-Old Boy*, Standard Edition, vol. X, ed. and trans. James Strachey (New York: W. W. Norton, 1955), pp. 3–149.

turned to females—for errant thoughts or feelings.) Hans's panic, however, showed method in its madness. The secondary gain of his symptoms effectively reunited him in the home with his love object: mother. He now could not (would not) leave her.

The psychosexual theory was a tremendous leap forward from the degenerate explanation of the day, and its validity is difficult to refute. What we might add, using new consciousness, is the recognition of gender roles that a young child becomes aware of at this time: his reaction to the expectation that those with a penis go out into the world whereas those without remain at home. Minimally, in the mind of a child seeing the giants out there, along with the tales he has been told, there might arise an ambivalence about being thrust into this dangerous, violent, and hostile environment.

Depending on his own understanding of the outside, whether based on self-perception or messages imposed, he might elect to remain in the confines of the female existence. These cultural subtleties are generally absent from Freud's formulations. Sadly, they continue to remain so in most of his followers..

Agoraphobia is clearly a woman's strategy. This is confirmed both historically and demographically. Yet that some men would use it, for different reasons or purposes, comes as no surprise. We recall that the Greek hero Achilles dressed in women's clothing when he wished to escape military service in the Trojan expedition. The same Achilles later withdrew from battle and sulked in his tent when he felt offended by Agamemnon.

In the case of agoraphobia, women and men are in general conversely motivated to stay at home. We believe that women remain housebound partially as a protest because they want access to the marketplace, men because the marketplace has lost its appeal. But in both instances they are responding to their own personal histories as well as to societal and cultural forces.

John, a man in his early fifties, came for therapy on the

advice of the Worker's Compensation Board because of complaints that were diagnosed as emotional problems. A chef by vocation, he had been unable to work for the past two years because he suffered excruciating and disabling bodily symptoms when he stepped out of his home. Physical examinations revealed no handicap; medical and psychological treatments, including hypnosis and various types of behavior modification therapy, did no good. He dated his difficulties to a dramatic episode that occurred while at work.

He related that he had worked as a chef at various restaurants since the age of sixteen. He had always been a hard and faithful worker and had consistently earned the praise of his employers in a high-tension business. However, at his last job, where he had worked steadily for three years, his boss, reacting to new competition in the neighborhood, was now placing the kitchen staff under heightened stress. Demands were made for quick changes in cooking practices and menus, greater economy, and the like.

One evening, with a large party in the dining room, the owner stormed into the kitchen and insisted on greater action from the beleaguered chef. John tried to explain that they were doing the best they could and uncharacteristically stood up to his employer. The owner struck him on the side of the face. The blow felled John, who tripped and hit his head against the foot of a stove. He suffered momentary unconsciousness and was taken to the emergency room of a hospital where he was examined and given a clean bill of health. There was no apparent injury other than some superficial bruises. John was told to go home, rest for a few days, and return to work. He went home and rested. But he never went back to his job.

During his first session, John described the miseries of being housebound. He was distraught by his inactive and useless life. He was ashamed; he was becoming like a woman. Always pious, he prayed three times a day that he would be relieved of his affliction. His cronies were impatient with him and his physical symptoms. "John," they said, "there is nothing wrong with you that work would not cure."

John pleaded with his doctors to be restored to his former self so that he could regain his self-respect and the respect of the people around him. But how could he work if he could not go through his front door without panic setting in? He had tried at least a dozen times to keep appointments with prospective employers; in most instances he never got beyond the house even when accompanied by his wife, relatives, or friends. On one occasion he did begin part-time work at a relative's restaurant, but after one day the palpitations, lightheadedness, and feelings of dread prevented his returning.

John's incapacitation was not confined to the routes to work; he was similarly unable to travel to most other public and private places. Although it required great effort, he could keep the doctor's appointments; if he were stricken in the doctor's office help was readily available.

John was born in Italy, an only child. His father was killed in an industrial accident when John was five. He was raised by his mother in extreme poverty and his formal education had been meager. When he was twelve, with the help of relatives he and his mother were able to come to this country.

His childhood contained little fun or playfulness. He worked at what he could to help his mother, and was devout to the point of superstition. (His mother had been the town's "faith-healer.") And although he was an extremely skilled chef, he never aspired, as was frequently suggested to him, to own his own place. He liked working for others. People would shake their heads and say, "John is always looking for a father." John responded: "I'll do my work and make good money. Let the bosses have the headaches."

It was John who ended up with the headache, an ache that would not go away. Whether the pain was caused by the humiliating slap from his boss, or by the accumulated humiliations of his entire life, we do not know. But we can be fairly sure about one thing: The only way for John the Chef to cease being a chef was to become too physically ill to participate in the man's world, the world of work.

The key to freedom, to health, for men is complex. The

messages that men have received since the beginning of time about worthiness have dealt uncompromisingly with strength, with toughness, with making money, with working. The solution for the man trying to slip out of the male role is not as simple as be weak, be gentle, don't make money, don't work.

A man in his early sixties came for psychotherapy because of isolation and friendlessness resulting, so he thought, from being diagnosed as mentally ill. Over the years of disabling emotional problems, he felt he had been abandoned by friends, relatives, the community. He had been going to a mental health clinic where treatment was largely a matter of giving him antidepressants. These drugs at times only added to his distress, making him too jittery at night to sleep, ruining the one element of his life that had been left unimpaired.

He had been married to the same woman for thirty-nine years and they had four grown children. He had had a lifetime of mental problems, which continue to this day. One constant nagging dread, he relates even at this age, was homosexuality. This despite his marriage and children and the fact that never since early adolescence had he engaged in sex with a man. Yet he is tortured by fantasies of homosexual activities, mainly fellatio. The sight of men in locker rooms and public toilets excites him; similarly, visits to the zoo or otherwise seeing the organs of male animals is a source of simultaneous excitement and terror. These thoughts and feelings have literally ruined his life; he cannot understand what they are or what they mean since by any standard of behavior and attitude, he knows that he is not, as he describes it, "queer."

By his own determinations, this obsession began forty years earlier when he was overseas in the army. He was assigned to kitchen detail as a cook's assistant. It was here that all his troubles began. Two of the other men in the kitchen were homosexual. This was his first experience with homosexuals and he was puzzled as well as chagrined by their behavior. In time they began taunting him and repeatedly tried to involve him in their activities. He resisted vehemently.

His sexual activities were solely with prostitutes. Yet the

two persisted their taunting and he developed severe physical symptoms—headaches, abdominal pains, general nervousness—that were eventually diagnosed as psychological.

After his discharge and return home, all of his symptoms miraculously disappeared. He looked back at his stint in the army as one prolonged nightmare. Now free of his two tormentors, he regained his health and attempted to resume a normal life. He soon fell in love, married, and settled down to have a family. Despite hard times he managed to find employment in a local steel mill where his father had worked.

His father had emigrated from eastern Europe, coming here out of extreme poverty. Finding employment as an iron worker and settling in a small mill town in upstate New York, he married a woman who had come from his village in Poland. When the patient was two years of age, his mother died in a flu epidemic. He has no memories of her. His father soon remarried but in a short time the new wife ran off with a boarder. Thereafter the boy was raised by a succession of hired housekeepers.

The father worked to keep the home together, but became a heavy drinker who often terrorized the household. The patient left school in the tenth grade; he was determined to leave this most unhappy household. Without training and unable to find work he enlisted in the army where he was confronted by still another travail.

After leaving the army, he felt lucky to get a job similar to his father's. It was hard work and, unlike his experience in the army kitchen, man's work. He did well there, feeling like a man among men. He received raises and promotions; he was made group leader by the union. At home his wife was loving and cooperative.

Just when all was going well, four men employees became antagonistic toward him. They would not work properly and tried to undercut his authority. They complained to other union officials about his leadership capabilities; they mocked his behavior. With this unexpected turn of events, the same physical symptoms that had plagued him in the army recurred.

Headaches and abdominal pains incapacitated him. No remedies helped and he was forced to quit his job. Again, he reflected, relationships with men undid him. This time, however, it was animosity with no sexual suggestion.

In comparing the two episodes, he began to ruminate on homosexuality. Was he homosexual himself? Were the men under him disobedient and defiant because they thought he was not a real man? He became obsessed with homosexual thoughts, abhorring them yet tormented by them.

When he was in the company of other men, he would find himself wondering about their penis sizes and whether they were in some way suggesting that he perform fellatio on them. Unemployed, beset by severe bodily complaints, tormented by alien thoughts, he became a recluse, hiding from other people—mainly other men—in whose presence these abominations would occur. The outside world contained evils; he became housebound.

He was cajoled into seeking psychiatric help. He related his physical distress but didn't mention the underlying obsessive thoughts. He was given antidepressants, which made things worse: Now he felt jittery at home, his only sanctuary. Discouraged and hopeless, he took an overdose. His wife found him in time and he was committed to a mental hospital. There he felt relatively secure, was placed on still more drugs, and after several months was discharged.

His course after being discharged from the hospital was stormy. Pressures toward "rehabilitation" began: Relatives, friends, and psychiatrists urged him to go back to work. Over a decade he had several jobs but each time he ended up trying to kill himself. No one could or would believe that he just wanted to be left alone, away from those dreaded stimulations.

The problem of homosexuality, and more specifically of homophobia, was but one facet, albeit the most obvious one, of a panoply of ambivalent feelings about the male world of aggression and competition, about the stereotypical male role that he was expected to assume. He had doubts as well about his emotional and intellectual preparation and capability to deal with the day-to-day male stresses, as well as with the more subtle power ploys and intrigues that go on in even the simplest work situations.

There is no question that his experience in the army, or more precisely, his utter lack of preparation for that experience, was traumatic. He had little formal education; what he knew of human behavior he learned at home or at church, the primary criterion being whether it was or was not sinful. Second to that was whether it was manly or feminine. Beyond these there were no alternatives, no possible options.

For any moment of compassion and understanding that might come his way, there were years of taunts and slurs. Hard work and honesty were often rewarded with envy and belittlement. He knew of abandonment, of death, of impoverishment of body and soul with no cogent explanation. These were out there where he was expected to be. In such circumstances he might well envy woman's confinement, despite the heavy price of such a violation of the masculine code.

He had no friends because he had joined the ranks of the mentally ill, surely nearly as contemptible as being a homosexual. The psychiatric treatment he received was a cruel imitation of his very disease and its causes. No explanations, just confinement and drugs. About the latter, he had painfully witnessed in his childhood how his father would lose his head with alcohol. He became befuddled and bewildered.

It is apparent that he suffered severely from homophobia. He is a prime example that the real homosexual problem in society today is not homosexuality but people's irrational feelings against it.

This patient's homosexuality was partially repressed, partially conscious, a state of mind that is known to produce a particular agony. He denied his obsession with the subject. He was stuck between floors, suffering discomfort and horror. Not only was he in agony over feelings he considered sinful, he was not in any way part of the homosexual community. And of course he was not sophisticated enough to participate in any kind of bisexual life-style. Repressed homosexuality is known to return to consciousness as distorted and dystonic. Freud used the word "acidulated" to describe this phenomenon.

This acidulation is derived from two thousand years of the most severe religious condemnation by God and man, an abomination that passed on to each generation, including our own. On this issue there is never an inch of cleavage between parent and pulpit; it is a mortal sin without exception or explanation.

Yet this young man was expected to play, train, sleep, work, and, if need be, die with other men, without ever experiencing passion or pleasure in the process.

We must take into account his extremely rigid upbringing, along with poor moral and secular education, which was characterized by arbitrary commands and prohibitions. This misfortune is suffered by so many who succumb to mental disturbances later in life; it is the curse of the inflexible or rigid superego, a mind from above, implanted rather than taught, held in place by threats, literal fire and brimstone.

For this patient the outside was the world of men. The sexual aspect was but one facet of a specter that held painful memories and defeats. Homosexuality was not the entire problem but a tangible and concrete issue on which to fasten his anxieties about men and work. It is more acceptable to fear the former than the latter: Working and competing with men in our society, for the male sex, is an unquestionable good.

After twelve years the patient became able to leave his home without experiencing panic and was thereby able to attend to some of the necessities of living. His obsession with homosexuality persisted but now exerted no great force. In Graham Greene's idiom we might call him a "burnt-out case." The reason that he could finally give up his self-imposed seclusion was probably that he had reached the age of retirement, so the issue of returning to work was moot. His chronic unhappiness continued; his friends shunned him. Yet better to be shunned because one is mentally ill than because one is a queer, a sinner.

This person probably never heard of Zarathustra or Nietzsche; nonetheless there is a striking parallel:

> Zarathustra spoke:
>
> Flee, my friend, into your solitude.
>
> When the market place begins . . . the buzzing of the poisonous flies begins too.
>
> Far from the market place and from fame happens all that is great; far from the market place and from fame the inventors of new values have always dealt.
>
> Flee unto your solitude! You have lived too close to the small and the miserable.
>
> Indeed, my friend, you are the bad conscience of your neighbors.
>
> . . . they hate you, therefore, and would like to suck your blood. Your neighbors will always be poisonous flies; that which is great in you, just that must make them more poisonous and more like flies.*

The patient had no special talents and nothing particularly great has or will come from him. Because of his ordinariness, any pretensions of greatness or separatist attitude based on purported superiority would automatically lead to a diagnosis of paranoid psychosis. Yet, in feeling people of all levels, there is a residual modicum of pride that induces a separation from those who insult and bludgeon. The man here stung by the flies of the marketplace could not return and yet understandably did not have the self-assurance to live apart from the community. For him, as for Nietzsche, the poisonous flies were other men.

In the instances of male agoraphobics we must include those who seem motivated by a need to preserve time and energy for the pursuit and development of nonvirile talents, which came in conflict with expected male behavior.

* Walter Kaufmann, ed. *The Portable Nietzsche* (New York: Penguin, 1977), p. 162.

Does the boy go outside to play baseball to fulfill his gender role expectations or does he remain within to practice the piano? This problem rarely exists for girls, as practicing the piano indoors prevails nine times out of ten (she could play baseball with the boys at the price of being called a tomboy). What if a boy has interests or talents that need a solitary ambience, for music or to write a poem? A boy today withdraws from sports at his peril. It may engender a conflict for which he has neither rhetoric nor solution but which may make the outdoors his personal enemy, an anathema, antagonistic to enclosures and solitude where flutes are played and poems written. He finds himself meeting the needs of societal gender expectations, and often powerless to do much about it.

Agoraphobia is rare among males. The outdoors is both the masculine preserve and imperative. Why would a male want to stay at home and, conversely, feel uncomfortable on the outside?

Time magazine reported on a touching and fascinating case: "For years, Manhattan Poet Joel Oppenheimer, now 47, took exactly the same route from his Greenwich Village apartment to his local bar, the Lion's Head. One day he tried a more circuitous route, walking along different streets. Midway to the bar he broke out in a cold sweat, suffering from heart palpitations, jelly legs and vertigo. 'I had no control over my body,' he said. 'It was total panic.'"

In the next paragraph we are told that "Crowds are no protection. Oppenheimer suffered one attack while surrounded by 55,000 fellow Mets fans at a playoff game." Fifty-five thousand fellow Mets fans indeed! What protection would they be to a poet? With the exception of "Casey at the Bat," poetry and baseball are inimical. A poet was a "swinger of birches" when they were still trees, not bats. Was Oppenheimer's creative conscience bothering him? Was it that he felt distressed to have allowed himself to become seduced and distracted by the banal excitements and temptations that gregariousness and games so amply and abundantly supply? Has anyone ever completed a poem in Shea Stadium? This is more apt to be done, if it is to be done, at home, safe. So for those whose talents require solitude and communication with the vast inside, the outer world with its macho imperatives and male-sanctioned distractions becomes a horrible danger.

We have taken many liberties with the article. Mr. Oppenheimer is not known to us nor has he been interviewed by us, so our analysis is gratuitous and based on the flimsiest of data. However, his case does resonate to a remarkable degree with phenomena generally observed in male agoraphobics: Most of them share an underlying conflict as to how much they can risk exposure to the distractions of the outer world as opposed to a limited and circumscribed environment where they can most profitably use their calling or talents. This conflict is inextricably tied to the masculine-feminine gender problem: A "real" man is fearless and adventuresome, loves the great out-of-doors as his primary arena, and probably shouldn't be indoors writing poetry.

We are on safer ground describing the case of a young man who came for therapy. A senior in college, in the last six months he had become panic-stricken outdoors. Driving his car became difficult; he was fearful of losing control and often had to return abruptly to his living quarters. His friends thought that he suffered from "graduation fever," fear of leaving the protection of the Alma Mater for worldly matters. It wasn't exactly that, though he did have a career problem. What future should he pursue? He loved music and was trained as a musician but his family, although sympathetic to his artistic bent, felt that music was no way to earn a living. They wanted him to seek a more traditional profession, perhaps the law, for which he had also shown some interest and aptitude. Socially he was friendly, likable, and affable—so much so that he had to guard his time against social intrusions and demands.

His developmental years were unexceptional but for one element: At an early age he began composing music. He came from a family with a musical background; music was frequently discussed and he was routinely given lessons. His parents were ambivalent about his precocity, loving music on the one hand but knowing also at first hand the vagaries of a musical career. They tempered their enthusiasm for this gift despite the encouragement of teachers and friends.

He continued writing for his own amusement; at the same time he did his academic work and perfunctorily played stickball as directed by his parents lest he become too studious. His family contained not only musicians but also several homosexuals. (His parents wanted a normal, healthy, well-rounded son, having seen enough of the fate of the sensitive, aesthetic types.) Yet in all, he recalls his childhood as a happy one, with seemingly little bearing on his present predicament.

As the psychoanalytic sessions proceeded, it became apparent that his symptoms reflected the dilemma between choosing a worldly, parent-accepted, manly calling and claiming as his own the activity that gave him so much challenge and pleasure. The pleasure of composing was an eminently somatic one; his body responded to the chords that went through his head and that he was then able to transpose through an instrument and on paper. During college he had the unique experience of a recital of his works.

His symptoms of street panic, although disturbing and restricting, indicated to him where he belonged and where the dangers of distractions lay. It was largely the success of the recital with its attendant acclaim that finally helped him abjure the practical path of law in favor of the visceral pull of music. His agoraphobia was a protective mechanism against the intrusions, temptations, and distinctions of the outer world. A clue to this came early in therapy when he mentioned his annoyance with anything that stole time away from him. He needed long periods for concentration on the internal stimuli that had to be attended. He was indeed an inside, internally directed person who knew he had to be on guard against the conventional and normative focus.

What was the outcome? After he decided to pursue a career in music, he became happier and "relieved." As he was gradually able to withdraw from the distractions of bores and boulevards, his attacks of panic largely disappeared. He was now able to say I prefer not going out, rather than I am afraid to go out. The victory of inner space over macho outer space rendered his neurosis unnecessary.

Robert Frost's preference for the boy "too far from town to learn baseball" is probably not understood by our determined polar gender experts; neither will be the next line: "Whose only play was what he found himself, Summer or Winter, and could play alone." Such a person has no need for a place like Shea Stadium.

Epilog

Eliminate metaphor from the law and you have
reduced its power to convince and convert.

Lon Fuller

Susan Sontag writes convincingly of our tendency historically to treat our organic diseases as metaphors and hold hapless victims personally and morally responsible for them. As
formerly people who fell ill were somehow thought to be "out
of grace," in the modern idiom various psychological states or
traumas are presented, albeit retrospectively, to explain afflictions. The new intellectual sophistication demanded that such
words as "trauma" and "psychopathology" replace such old-
fashioned phrases as "fallen from Grace" and "wages of sin."
The metaphors then become extended as objectives for a host
of social, economic, and political scourges. Watergate became
the "cancer on the Presidency." Sontag recalls calling the
Vietnam war the "cancer of Asia." These expressions add
moral burdens to the people who are the actual victims of
these diseases, literally adding insult to injury. Patients have
to bear the onus wrought by this literary license.

While Sontag decries treating disease as metaphor, the
converse is happening with such conditions as agoraphobia—
metaphors are being treated as diseases. The agoraphobic is a
living and acting metaphor, making a statement, registering a
protest, effecting a sit-in strike, enacting a parody and a caricature. Just as we mistakenly impart motivation to the patient
with a physical disease, we deny it to the agoraphobic. We see

209

the latter condition as bereft of meaning and content, thereby justifying surgery, chemotherapy, psychotherapy, and all types of conditioning and reconditioning.

What's to be done to a metaphor? In whose province does it fall? Is it to be left alone as an expressive device, or treated as a disease by a physician? Or should an English teacher deal with it?

Imagine a conversation. One person, illustrating a daredevil exploit of a friend says, "He burned his bridges behind him." The listener replies with seriousness: "That reminds me of what happened to us as we traveled south. We saw a car on fire on the Brooklyn Bridge. We helped extinguish it." If all parties present, for whatever reasons, decide to talk about bridges instead of the subject at hand, we get an inkling of what happens when the metaphor is treated, as is the case with agoraphobia. A person is trying to describe cryptically a feeling or attitude held and often reflected through modes of behavior, his anxiety about *crossing* bridges. Suddenly the metaphor is eclipsed and bridges become the issue. The person, now client or patient, is to be desensitized or treated so that she can deal with bridges. This literal, impersonal approach is the state of the art today. It is accepted that the agoraphobic is expressing nothing more than fear of the street or love of home. Not only is it accepted, it is actively promoted.

In speaking of metaphor as disease we are, of course, articulating the very human mental attribute of symbolization, that magnificent shorthand that has made all of our worldly achievements possible. Without the use of symbols and the symbolic process our tasks would be so laborious and cumbersome that we would never get through the day. Symbols generally stand for ideas and people; chaos results when the symbol and what it stands for are not understood. For instance, it would be the height of folly to die for the nation's flag, to expose oneself to murderous gunfire if one sees that it has fallen from its perch. But it is understandable and perhaps reasonable to die for what it stands for—home, nationhood, liberty, freedom—as people have done throughout history.

The agoraphobic patient's symptoms are reactions to symbols that stand for ideas and concepts largely hidden. Yet these symbols and reactions retain a semblance of and are clues to the original concept and idea that they represent. Psychiatrist Sylvano Arieti explains that the phobic patient "concretizes" a more general anxiety situation or idea complex that must be hidden, even from the self: "Fear of sexual relations hides a bigger fear in sustaining love relationships; fear of travel hides a bigger fear of making excursions into life; fear of many little things generally hides a general state of insecurity."* Always behind the object feared hides a concept, an idea, or a conviction that at the time cannot be faced. What an exercise in futility and how antipsychological are the treatments directed at the concretization rather than at the ideas or thoughts behind them. At a primitive level this can be temporarily pleasing to some patients, for it helps to disguise and to distract. Ultimately, however, it serves to diminish hope about the prospects for real problem-solving, especially if the therapist too becomes engaged in looking for the half-dollar under the streetlamp.

Consonant with the personal liberties of an open society, agoraphobes should not be coerced into places and activities from which they have obviously recoiled. Relatives, friends, and therapists in this regard should avoid intruding into their lives any more than into those engaged in mourning or meditation. Therapy is not therapy if it is involuntary, coercive, and intrusive. Here prescribing and proscribing have no place; the problems of women will not be solved by additional domination, mystification, and trivialization. Those who purport to be helpful should instead worry about their own ethical behavior and the demands of good manners. Therapeutic zeal must never take precedence over respect. Therapists, counselors, and aides must understand that agoraphobes have no physical paralysis and really do not have to be taught to walk on the

* "A Re-examination of the Phobic Symptom and of Symbolism in Psychotherapy," *American Journal of Psychiatry*, 118 (August 1961): 106–10.

street—certainly not by snapping rubber bands or stalking pipe cleaners. And drugging them to change their behavior must be recognized as just that, therapeutic euphemisms notwithstanding. The agoraphobe has not accepted second-class status and must not be forced to do so.

If a dialogue with a therapist is ultimately possible after a proper explication and sharing of understanding, the agoraphobe may make changes in her own life making broader existence more palatable. This would depend to a large measure on opportunities that are available. But as important as the personal equation are efforts directed toward promoting fair play and justice for her sex in the marketplace as well as in the home. This means a consciousness and involvement in women's issues, which, as we perceive it, were the chief contributors to her cynicism. This inevitably entails an active, often public struggle for social and cultural changes. When it can be done, the expenditure of energies toward a truly liberating goal provides the basis for *hope*—for oneself and others. There can be no better cure.

We perceive the agoraphobe as seemingly succumbing to, but in fact vigorously protesting, societal intimidation, sex-role stereotypes, and oppression. Although men too are found here, it is primarily women's way of fighting back. Demographic studies make it clear: Only in pregnancy is the prevalence of women greater. Agoraphobes, more sensitive than the general population, demand equal participation or they will not participate at all. Perhaps they are stubborn and uncompromising—a disease in itself. They are not good at adapting to a reality that they perceive as inequitable and unjust. They caricature the pitiful role assigned to them in which their legitimate strivings are as thwarted and unfulfilled as they are unrevealed and unspoken. Yet agoraphobes, in their so-called neuroticism, are acting out a strong personal political statement about their own plight in a restrictive society. True to the nature of political statements, an inherent duplicity is also displayed in the service of achieving and deceiving.

Again the agoraphobe follows political practice: Don't listen to what we say, watch what we do. Politicians know that full candor often brings defeat to worthy causes. Thus the agoraphobe speaks publicly of her "noble" motives of wanting only to adapt and to cooperate, to fulfill her role as good wife and good mother. She expresses shame about her own inadequacies in not being able to venture forth like "normal people."

But normal people are not society's protesters. They go along, make the necessary adaptive compromises, and never bring changes. "Normal" women have for centuries accepted oppression and imprisonment within their houses, making a virtue of their confinement. Women left their houses as the male world permitted and as they themselves acquiesced to the restrictive covenants imposed. Similarly, normal people accepted and were resigned to sexual role assignment and stereotyping that had nothing at all to do with sex or merit, but represented a massive exploitation.

Agoraphobes never speak of protest or politics; they speak of their medical and bodily symptoms. They know only too well the dangers of public political pronouncements, our alleged constitutional guarantees notwithstanding. For the United States Constitution, like the laws governing other nations, does not extend the usual guarantees of human rights to women. Attempts to remedy this discrepancy since 1920 have encountered ruthless opposition.

The agoraphobe alone is an unreconstructed idealist: Women have always been well tolerated as hysterics and hypochondriacs, but never politically. Ask Joan of Arc. It is no accident that agoraphobes become the property of our clinicians rather than becoming our political leaders. Both historically and contemporarily, it has been safer for women to have medical complaints than political grievances. Our clinicians do a land-office business in punishment and pejoration.

Those in the helping professions will not go outside the home to find and investigate the forces operative in this "disease" that they so vigorously treat. They continue to diagnose to suit their remedies. By their therapies they serve to reaffirm to the agoraphobe just how oppressive the male-dominant society really is.

The agoraphobe, using the clinicians, easily proves that she is not paranoid. With but minimal effort on her part she can get them to drug, incarcerate, lobotomize, humiliate, trivialize, and ridicule, as well as run roughshod over any remaining human right. This submission is not feminine masochism. It is a most subtle aspect of passive resistance by playing the feminine role. By complete acquiescence the agoraphobe becomes the complete homebody.

Agoraphobes may end their sit-in strikes following practices in labor disputes in general. Either the penalties for striking become unbearable or the situation changes in favor of the striking workers. The strike of the agoraphobe hinges on the shifting tides of her existence.

Women sadly have been forced to give the appearance of being against themselves. A strong and influential queen found it necessary to use the rhetoric of pretense and deference in the performance of her duties. Recently in the United States forceful, intelligent women pathetically use their energies to defeat the amendment to the Constitution that would promote equity between women and men. Both instances demonstrate the extent of the coercion, tragically internalized, brought to bear on the purported weaker sex.

Hysteria, so exclusively a woman's defense, may be viewed as a direct manifestation of this insidious oppression. The great hope for her personal emotional well-being resides in the overall social and cultural improvement of women's lot. We might safely predict that as these changes occur in our institutions, agoraphobia will disappear just as conversion hysteria has become a rarity. This followed women's gaining greater control over their own bodies and functions, especially in matters of sexual behavior and reproduction. As a result, no longer can psychiatry produce its parade of women with feigned motor paralysis, mock sensory disturbances, and other obscure bodily dysfunctions. One recalls that psychoanalysis cut its eyeteeth on such stuff but never really wondered why there had to be an intensive search to find similar occurrences among men.*

The forefront of social changes will be in the area of childrearing, breaking away from those stereotypes that lay the groundwork for the gross inequities that surface later in life. Second, the anachronisms of marriage must undergo badly needed corrections to make it worthy of a mutually fulfilling relationship and a valid model for children. And, lastly, in the *agora* the benefits and responsibilities of a meritorious and egalitarian society must be fully and genuinely extended to women. Then there will be little need for subterfuge, deception, and caricature.

* Sigmund Freud, "Report on My Studies in Paris and Berlin," Standard Edition, vol. I, ed. and trans. James Strachey (New York: W. W. Norton, 1966), pp. 1–15, and "Observation of a Severe Case of Hemi-Anaesthesia in a Hysterical Male," pp. 23–31.

INDEX

About the Authors

Robert Seidenberg, M.D., is a practicing psychiatrist and psychoanalyst in Syracuse, New York. He is Clinical Professor of Psychiatry at the Upstate Medical Center, State University of New York. A founder and past president of the Western New York Psychoanalytic Society, he is a certified member of the American Psychoanalytic Association and a life fellow of The American Psychiatric Association. He is also on the board of consulting editors of *Voices*, a journal published by the American Academy of Psychotherapists. Dr. Seidenberg has written and lectured extensively on the importance and relevance of feminist insights in the understanding of psychiatric entities. In this regard he has focused on the problem of uprooting in corporate life and on the prescription mind-drug assault on women patients.

Karen DeCrow is an attorney in Syracuse, New York, specializing in constitutional, literary, and entertainment law. She was the national president of the National Organization for Women (NOW) from 1974 to 1977. A graduate of the Medill School of Journalism, Northwestern University, and the Syracuse University College of Law, she was the first woman to run for mayor of Syracuse. Her articles have appeared in *Vogue, Mademoiselle, The New York Times,* the *Los Angeles Times,* the *Boston Globe,* and the *Miami Herald.* Karen De-Crow was voted one of the fifty most influential women in America by the Newspaper Enterprise Association and she was chosen by *Time* magazine as one of the two hundred future leaders of America.